PREACHING FROM PROPHETIC BOOKS

PREACHING
FROM
PROPHETIC BOOKS

ANDREW WATTERSON BLACKWOOD

ABINGDON-COKESBURY PRESS
New York • Nashville

PREACHING FROM PROPHETIC BOOKS

COPYRIGHT MCMLI
BY PIERCE AND SMITH

Scripture quotations unless otherwise designated are from the American Standard Version, copyright renewal 1929 by the International Council of Religious Education.

SET UP, PRINTED, AND BOUND BY THE PARTHENON PRESS, AT NASHVILLE, TENNESSEE, UNITED STATES OF AMERICA

FOREWORD

THIS BOOK DEALS WITH THE PULPIT USE OF PROPHETIC writings. It has grown out of my earlier volume, *Preaching from the Bible*. Unlike most works about the prophets, this one has to do with preaching values rather than matters of criticism and exegesis. All of that ought to interest every student and teacher of the Bible. But why should such a book as this deal sketchily with what the reader can find in full elsewhere? Also, why have a literary shop stocked with secondhand goods? For many things we who deal with practical theology must rely largely on the researches of scholars. So this book has to do only with preaching values.

Thanks are extended to the faculty of Bethel Theological Seminary, Cumberland Presbyterian Church, McKenzie, Tennessee, who invited me to deliver the first series of Johns Lectures, out of which this book has grown; to professors and librarians at Princeton Seminary, Temple University, and various other schools of theology; to Montreat, Lake Junaluska, and other Bible conferences; to my many students, past and present; and to countless pastors, near and far. The Fleming H. Revell Company

5

has given special permission to draw freely from my early book for laymen, *The Prophets: Elijah to Christ.* All of these have helped me more than they can know.

No one has ever discovered a short cut to mastery of prophetic writings. Neither should anyone hand out materials ready for use in the pulpit, like "pie mix." This work aims rather to promote intelligent study and use of prophetic oracles, one book at a time. Would that the treatment might include Elijah, Jonah, and Daniel;[1] also Joel, Zechariah, and Malachi. As for Obadiah and Nahum, Zephaniah and Haggai, let the pulpit interpreter keep to the main stream of prophecy. More important still, would that this work had more to do with eschatology, as the times demand today. But that would call for another volume, far harder to prepare. Meanwhile this work points out abundant opportunities for the daily use of a man's own pick and shovel, with constant help from such works as appear in the *Related Readings.*

Everywhere the book takes for granted that the active preparation of a sermon ought to start with a vision of human need in the home community today, and that every local church ought to enjoy a popular teaching ministry. In a recent Lyman Beecher Lecture at Yale, Miss Helen Kenyon, lay moderator of the Congregational Christian Church, voiced the feelings of many church-

[1] For brief discussions of Elijah, Jonah, and Daniel, see my *Preaching from the Bible* (New York and Nashville: Abingdon-Cokesbury Press, 1941), pp. 81-85, 85-88, 176-78.

goers today. After sixty years of regular church attendance she can remember little that she has learned from the pulpit. Hence she advises ministers, "Give us more teaching and less preaching." She also urges pastors to "water down their learned preaching so that the people in the pews can share their thinking." [2] What words of wisdom for any minister, especially when preaching from the prophets!

More messages full of divine grace and human interest! More sermons about the lives of men today in the light of God's written Word! More pulpit work meaty in substance and simple in style, well cooked and served warm! If anyone asks how he can prepare such a meal of food from the prophets, the reply must vary according to the needs of the hearers, the personality of their pastor, and the character of the prophetic book. No two churches today need the same diet; no two interpreters ought to work the same way; no two prophetic oracles call for the same treatment. Fortunately, the same Holy Spirit who led each of the prophets to write in a fashion all his own, stands ready now to guide the interpreter in meeting the needs of men and women in our days full of uncertainty and dread. Whenever a man preaches, let him declare, "Thus saith the Lord!"

ANDREW WATTERSON BLACKWOOD

[2] See the *New York Times*, April 21, 1950, p. 21.

CONTENTS

I

VII
Jeremiah

VIII
Habakkuk

IX
Ezekiel

X

CHAPTER I

THE PROPHETS AS GREAT PREACHERS

ANY LIST OF MASTER PREACHERS OUGHT TO GIVE FIRST place to the Hebrew prophets. Except when we refer to God, we ought seldom to employ the word great, but how else can we appraise such preachers as Amos and Hosea, or Isaiah and Jeremiah? At least I have come to this conclusion. Years ago I made a study of the prophetic writings. Since then I have lived with many other preachers whom the Church counts great, or near great. Now I come back to the prophets as the greatest of all, excepting only our Lord and two of His apostles.

How does a student of preaching estimate greatness? Chiefly by a man's influence after the conditions that surround him have passed away. In study of both history and literature we have learned the value of such a long view. Instead of beginning with such influence, however, let us first think about the prophets themselves and about the written reports of their sermons. In order to account for later influence we may think of four different factors. If anyone wishes to add still other tests, no doubt he will arrive at the same conclusion.

GREATNESS OF PERSONALITY AS PREACHERS

These mighty men illustrate the well-known description of preaching as divine truth voiced by a chosen personality to meet the needs of men in his day. Personality may mean all that the Lord gives an interpreter to make him one of Carlyle's "speaking men." Such descriptions fall short of the facts. No set of words can body forth the meaning of personality or preaching. So let an artist present the facts as they have to do with the personalities of the prophets, the mightiest preachers in history.

In a frieze at the Boston Public Library, John S. Sargent painted these men of old as living characters. He may have caught the spirit of Isaiah or Hosea better than that of Jeremiah or Amos. Even so, the painter assembled in a single group an array of preaching talent unmatched in any other painting. Except in the figure of our Lord, not even da Vinci's portrayal of the "Last Supper" presents such commanding personalities as those in Sargent's frieze of the prophets. A copy should hang on the study wall of every young minister to remind him that in the preaching of God's truth nothing on the human level bulks so large as personality, and that in its upper reaches personality appears in the prophets, who were supreme among earth's preachers.

Unfortunately, four of the prophets have become known as major, and twelve as minor, labels that have come down from Augustine of Hippo. As every reader knows, these labels refer only to the length or brevity of prophetic books. As they appear in our English Bible, the first four run longer than any of the other twelve. The list of sixteen does not include other seers, such as Elijah and Elisha, though the Hebrews looked on Elijah as the greatest of all their seers. Like many a strong preacher in our own time, this man left no volume of sermons, but still he deserves a seat among the mighty. So do Amos, Hosea, and perhaps one or two other minor prophets rank with the major four.

In our own time men have made a similar grouping of our Presidents, though with more classifications. Fifty-five of the country's leading historians have contributed to a composite list of chief executives not now living.[1] Six of the Presidents appear as "great," four as "near great," eleven as "average," six as "below average," and two as "failures." In like manner a group of Bible scholars could make a composite list of the prophets on the basis of their lasting influence as preachers. These students of comparative greatness would have to do with men mightier than our Presidents. The comparative ratings of the various prophets would encourage younger ministers to become acquainted with the greatest of all preachers.

Any such grouping would ignore the fact that each of those holy men differed from all the others, as "one star

[1] For the list see A. M. Schlesinger, *Paths to the Present* (New York: The Macmillan Co., 1949), pp. 95-96.

13

differeth from another star in glory." As we have already noted, each man's written work calls for a different approach, and the use of a different method. In making ready to preach from a prophetic book how can anyone decide on the best approach and the best method of study? Only by making a careful study of the prophet as he appears in the history of his time, and then by living with his book until the interpreter senses its "tone color." In some such fashion many of us have tried to approach and master the plays of Shakespeare. We could not use the same method with *Henry the Fifth* as with *Twelfth Night,* or with *Twelfth Night* as with *Macbeth.*

But why should we think of the prophetic books on such a human level? Why not frankly accept the fact of their inspiration, and in that truth rejoice? Indeed, we ought to think of the prophets themselves as inspired. "In many and various ways God spoke of old to our fathers by the prophets; but in these last days he has spoken to us by a Son." (Heb. 1:1-2*a* R.S.V.) "No prophecy ever came by the impulse of man, but men moved by the Holy Spirit spoke from God." (II Pet. 1:21 R.S.V.) Before this holy mystery of revelation and inspiration we ought to bow down and adore. Even if we cannot understand, at least we can rejoice in the light of God that has come through the prophets of old.

14

THE PROPHETS AS GREAT PREACHERS

GREATNESS OF MESSAGE AS PREACHERS

We today often think more of the human personality than of the message from God. Not so with the prophets of old! They looked on themselves first of all as men with a message from above, and on the truths that they proclaimed as more important by far than the interpreters. These men excelled as statesmen and reformers, as poets and orators, as teachers and counselors. Above all, in their own sight as in that of God, they spoke as interpreters of life in their day, in light that came from the God of all the days.

This idea of the prophets first of all as preachers calls for emphasis through repetition. Amid all the flood of books about these men, few have dealt with them first of all as preachers. Here and there a scholar has called attention to what the prophets themselves always kept central. For example, a scholar of yesterday anticipated the best thinking of our time about this part of the Old Testament:

The prophets were evangelistic preachers. . . . Most of the prophetic books are volumes either of sermons or of homiletical books or tracts. In many instances a passage in the prophets becomes intelligible only when we recognize it as a syllabus or brief sketch of an address that was much longer when delivered orally.[2]

[2] See Willis J. Beecher, *The Prophets and the Promise* (New York: Crowell, 1905), p. 99.

The word "prophet" means forth-teller, and not for-
tuneteller. The term itself comes from the Greek by
transliteration. The correct usage of the word appears in
Exod. 7:1, where the Lord speaks to Moses: "I have made
thee as God to Pharaoh; and Aaron thy brother shall be
thy prophet"—"one who speaks on behalf of another."
Sometimes the spokesman reveals the will of God concerning the past, and again about the future. As a rule he
interprets the present. Whatever the period of time he
holds in view, he always relates the message to the interests
and the needs of the hearers. Partly for this reason many
a prophetic oracle becomes clear and luminous only after
the interpreter has become familiar with the background
in history.

What, then, did these men preach? In terms of today
they presented doctrine and duty. The doctrine had to do
first of all and most of all with God. Amos with his
"ethical monotheism," Isaiah with the stress on holiness,
and all the others with their contributions to the understanding of God—these men laid deep and strong the
foundations of what we now know as biblical theology.
The doctrines also had to do with the sins of men and
with the oncoming of judgment. Especially in Isaiah and
in Micah the prophetic teachings about the Kingdom of
God culminated in promises about the coming Messiah.
Now that seminary professors and local pastors everywhere have begun anew to stress the theology of the Bible,

they ought to see that under God it nearly all stems from the writings of the prophets.

On the basis of what they believed about God the prophets also dealt largely and boldly with ethics. At times such men as Elijah and Amos, or Isaiah and Micah, may have seemed to proclaim little else than ethics. They insisted that the character of God ought to determine the conduct of His followers. Sometimes, as with Elijah before King Ahab, the high ethical teaching had to do with the will of God for one man alone in the presence of the Eternal. More often, as with Amos the herdsman at sophisticated Bethel, the prophet stressed the will of God for the people as a whole. Never since those ancient times has any group of men produced a body of ethical teachings so all-inclusive and so heart-searching. Today when we refer to our pulpit ministry as prophetic, do we understand that the term calls for both doctrine and duty? They in turn require both wisdom and courage.

So we might run through our homiletical labels, only to find that many of them fit the prophetic writings, at least loosely. Think of Amos at Bethel delivering an occasional sermon; Isa. 40, a pastoral message, "Comfort ye, comfort ye my people"; Isa. 55, like many another prophetic oracle, evangelistic, "Seek ye the Lord while he may be found"; Jeremiah's use of the case method in preaching about the ways of the potter; Habakkuk's life-situation sermon about the conversion of an honest doubter; Malachi's reliance on a teaching ministry. So we might go on, but let us understand that the prophets would not have cared for such labels.[3] Unlike some of us, they did not "preach for the salvation of their sermons."

In short, think of the prophets as men with a message from God. If any reader wishes to make a study of preaching, let him begin at the fountainhead, with the Hebrew prophets. Better still, if anyone desires to become a stronger preacher, let him live with these masters of old, one at a time. In the history of the Church almost every man who has excelled as a preacher has at some time sat at the feet of some pulpit master. Where can any young aspirant find nobler exemplars than among these ancient worthies? Where can he find better materials for case studies than in these prophetic oracles? All the while let him remember that the value and the power lie far more in the message than in the preacher, and that the message comes from God. No wonder we think much about "the mystery of preaching"!

GREATNESS OF STYLE AS PREACHERS

Any student of world literature should agree that in literary form the writings of the prophets surpass the sermonic work of every other group. Even in translation many of their words sing their way into the soul and there

---

[3] For the limitations of our labels see my *Preparation of Sermons* (New York and Nashville: Abingdon-Cokesbury Press, 1948), pp. 27-34.

keep echoing the holiness of our God and the wonders of redeeming grace. The haunting melody of their words rings out still more wondrously in the Hebrew original. There the parallelism differs from anything else in the world of books, so that if only for their beauty and power as literature, the world would not willingly let the prophetic writings disappear.

If such a lofty estimate seems extreme, try an experiment. For an hour or two read aloud from the most familiar chapters in the prophetic books, being sure to bring out the heartthrobs as they appear in the Hebrew rhythm. Then pick up a collection of more recent sermons,[4] and do much the same with messages that you esteem most highly. If you know how to read, and how to bring out the music that lies hidden in words, you will feel that you have come down from the heights where the prophets dwell with God and that you move among the foothills from which you can view the Alpine heights afar off. Good as you may find more than a few recent sermons, you cannot compare them with the prophetic oracles, which tower aloft "like the Matterhorn, unmatched in all the world."

The prophets could speak and write with power and majesty because they had the souls of poets. In the newer versions of the Old Testament much of the prophetic writings appears in the form of verse, but for some reason

[4] See my *Protestant Pulpit* (New York and Nashville: Abingdon-Cokesbury Press, 1947).

19

the words do not flow so smoothly as in the old King James Version or in Martin Luther's German Bible. Fortunately, no literalistic rendering can obscure or dim the beauty and splendor of the prophetic writings at their best. However, not all of the prophets could qualify as poets. In the newer versions large parts of Jeremiah, Ezekiel, and Zechariah stand out as prose.

As poets and preachers these mighty men of old show us how to use imagination for the glory of the God from whom it comes. Of them and their writings Horace Bushnell might have written what he did about the gospel as "the gift of God to the imagination." [5] The term here means God-given ability to see what lies hidden from other eyes, and then to use words in helping others to behold the "vision splendid." If the prophets did nothing more for the interpreter today, they should at least set his imagination at work among the truths of God. Why not resolve to live with them, one by one, until your horizon broadens?

> The world stands out on either side
>   No wider than the soul is wide;
> Above the world is stretched the sky,—
>   No higher than the soul is high.
> The heart can push the sea and land
>   Farther away on either hand;

[5] See the essay in *Building Eras in Religion* (New York: Charles Scribner's Sons, 1881).

The soul can split the sky in two,
  And let the face of God shine through.
But East and West will pinch the heart
  That can not keep them pushed apart;
And he whose soul is flat—the sky
  Will cave in on him by and by.[6]

GREATNESS OF INFLUENCE AS PREACHERS

According to students of world literature greatness shows itself chiefly in power that continues to work after the conditions that produced the writings have passed away. Through the personality and the message of such a preacher as Amos or Isaiah the Spirit of God has caused many a truth to prevail until the present hour. Hence the brilliant German scholar Carl H. Cornill could speak of prophecy as "one of the greatest spiritual forces that the history of mankind has ever witnessed." Again he declared: "The whole history of mankind has nothing that can be compared in the remotest degree with the prophecy of Israel." [7] In our own time a Canadian scholar has written much the same: "The supreme spiritual achievement of the prophets was that they founded the religion of hope, and gave to the world, to the restless movements

[6] Edna St. Vincent Millay, "Renascence," *Renascence and Other Poems* (New York: Harper & Bros.). Copyright 1912, 1940 by Edna St. Vincent Millay. Reprinted by permission of Brandt & Brandt, New York.

[7] See *The Prophets of Israel*, Eng. ed. (Chicago: Open Court Publishing Co., 1897), p. 197.

21

of men, and to the destiny of individuals, a center in God." [8]

Most of all these men of God influenced the writers of the New Testament. According to Cornill, "Jesus of Nazareth linked His own activity to the prophecy of ancient Israel, Himself the purest blossom and fairest flower." So did almost every writer of a New Testament book carry on the prophetic tradition and ideals. Throughout the New Testament, according to the best scholarship of our day, the kerygma serves as the ground plan. This kerygma, or message from God, comes from the Old Testament, and chiefly from the prophetic books. As the heart and center of the gospel it provides the substance of all that we Christians can preach today.[9]

During the Middle Ages these oracles often found a secondary place, if not one lower down. Except in the way of allegorical fancies these parts of Holy Writ seldom appeared in the pulpit. At the Reformation, with its emphasis on expository work from both Testaments, the prophets again came into their own, not least with John Calvin as an interpreter. In our own day they bid fair once again to assume their place of honor as the most important and fruitful parts of the Old Testament, side by side with the Psalms. Meanwhile the Church waits for a

[8] See R. B. Y. Scott, *The Relevance of the Prophets* (New York: The Macmillan Co., 1944), p. 197.
[9] For a discussion of the kerygma see C. H. Dodd, *The Apostolic Preaching and Its Developments* (New York: Harper & Bros., 1950).

generation of young ministers who can open up the treasures that lie hidden in these prophetic mines.

From this point onward we shall keep thinking chiefly about the prophetic oracles as sources of preaching material, and not about the men as preachers. Naturally the one line of thought will often lead into the other. Largely because these men of God knew what to preach, and how, they have given us endless resources of truth and grace.

If you would appraise these men, try a practical experiment extending over eight or ten years. Plan to live with eight or ten of the prophets and their books, mastering at least one of the books each year. Begin with one of the simplest, such as Micah or Amos. Become well acquainted with the man and his writings. Learn all you can about his message as it concerned the men of his own time, and as it applies today. After months of fellowship with such a master spirit prepare a number of consecutive morning or evening sermons from this one prophetic source.

After a man has kept up this kind of Bible study and interpretation for eight or ten years, he will understand why those who know the prophets best revere them most, and why many of us love to sing at the ordination of a young minister:

> God of the prophets! Bless the prophets' sons:
>   Elijah's mantle o'er Elisha cast;
> Each age its solemn task may claim but once:
>   Make each one nobler, stronger than the last!

23

Chapter II

Amos

THE VOICE OF GOD'S RIGHTEOUSNESS

Among all the prophets no one deserves to rank higher than Amos. According to Cornill, a distinguished scholar of yesterday, this prophet stood out as "one of the most marvelous and incomprehensible figures in the history of the human mind." In the words of a present-day scholar this "first in the line of the great reforming prophets . . . changed the center of gravity in religion from the externally correct to the internally moral." For Amos religion consisted "not in ritual but in righteousness." His work marked "the beginning of a new era in the history of religions." [1] In short, the most creative and the most influential of all the prophetic writers! What an achievement for a country preacher from the hills who knew nothing of culture in the schools!

Even more than other seers, Amos lived and spoke as a son of God's outdoors. He dwelt among the wilds and spoke in terms of wide open spaces. Amos belonged in Tekoa, a hamlet five miles south of Bethlehem. The region

---

[1] Excerpts from Robert H. Pfeiffer, *Introduction to the Old Testament* (New York: Harper & Bros., 1948), pp. 580-82.

24

round Tekoa, known as a desert, was to become the scene of preaching by John the Baptist, and of the devil's tempting our Lord. Among rugged hills that others would think Godforsaken, Amos herded cattle, which may have belonged to another man. To eke out a living the future interpreter also pruned sycamore trees. When he wrote this book, he showed a love of the land, with a knowledge of wild beasts. Better still, out among the fields he had come to know God.

This prophet, reared in the Southern Kingdom, seems to have spoken only in the Northern. He may have expected to end his days among his own bleak hills, but he heard the call of God to preach at Bethel. There among the elite of the land he showed the strength and courage he had previously displayed in rescuing from the mouth of a lion two legs of a calf and a piece of the ear. Like Moses, this other seer had lived so long in the wilds of earth that he had caught much of her simplicity and grandeur. In strength and in vividness his writings hold their own with those of Isaiah. Even in English, and much more in Hebrew, his written work "preserves all the effects of pointed and dramatic delivery, with the breadth of lyrical fervor that lends a charm to the highest Hebrew oratory." [2]

Amos went to prophesy in Bethel about 760 B.C. during the reign of Jeroboam II. In less than twoscore years that

---

[2] See R. F. Horton, *The Minor Prophets*, "New Century Bible" (New York: Frowde, 1906), p. 122.

Northern Kingdom would go into captivity. For the nonce, however, partly because of peace with neighboring lands, Israel seemed to enjoy the utmost prosperity in her history. For a time near-by Syria left her alone, and more distant Assyria had not begun to affright. While Israel prospered, her blessings did not extend down to the so-called lower classes. The rich kept building among the hills summer homes full of splendor, and in the city winter houses adorned with ivory. There they lolled on silken couches made possible by grinding the faces of the poor. According to Amos, "they have sold the righteous for silver, and the needy for a pair of shoes. They pant after the dust of the earth on the heads of the poor." The upper classes, so-called, also indulged in impurity and kindred vices, all unashamed.

Those people gave a large place to "religion," much of which centered at Bethel. There they assembled at a "high place"—one set apart for idolatrous worship. In Bethel and in Dan, Jeroboam I had established high places as the foci round which the religious life of the Northern Kingdom would revolve. Bethel soon drew many patrons away from Dan. Although not the capital city, Bethel seems to have become the largest and strongest center in Israel. There the priests and the false prophets made their homes, with many others who craved the consolations of an easygoing cult. To Bethel as a shrine hosts of God's professed children flocked at times to bask in the radiance of a religion that had little to say about their sins.

The public worship of that "state church" consisted largely in "baptized paganism"—costly, splendid, hollow. Even when offered in the name of the Lord God, that worship came in forbidden forms. It wrought no transformation in the hearts and lives of men and women. Indeed, it fostered every sort of physical and moral uncleanness. Surely Bethel needed to hear a spokesman from the Most High. No less surely, she felt no need of such a message. Hence this chapter might bear the heading, "God's Warning to a Complacent People." The same would hold true today in more than one city that prides itself on the number of people who take part in the public worship of God.

Our rural seer may have come to Bethel on a feast day. When he began to speak, he must have caused a commotion. Not only did he stand out as a son of Judah, twin sister of Israel and her constant rival. Amos must also have worn the roughest garb, and have spoken in a rugged way that would jar the nerves of Bethel, whose prophets prided themselves on seeming smooth. Think of John the Baptist at the court of King Herod or of Savonarola among the elite of Florence. How could a herdsman from the hills of Judah gain a hearing in the religious center of her northern rival, and that on a day set apart for godless mirth? Would he launch forth in a tirade against the sins

27

of Israel? No, he began with a psychological approach that would serve as a model for any diplomat today.

THE SINS OF THE NATIONS (1:1–4:3)

Like a missionary abroad, the prophet began with truths the hearers accepted gladly. Instead of arousing animosity by attacking the sins of his hearers, Amos denounced the cruelties of surrounding nations. In doing so he massed the materials most carefully. Starting with Syria he pointed out the enormities of one nation after another. Next to the last he came to Judah, the most closely related of Israel's neighbors. "I will send a fire upon Judah, and it shall devour the palaces of Jerusalem." What glee Amos must have brought those leaders of Israel! But wait! He has one word more, and this to Israel herself.

"For three transgressions of Israel, yea, for four, I will not turn away the punishment thereof." This refrain, which had sounded like sweet music when it told of Israel's enemies, must have stricken terror to those people who at last stood face to face with their own sins. What could they plead in self-defense? Had they not acclaimed the justice of God in dealing with nations guilty of barbarism? At last they could see that Israel had committed more dastardly sins of "civilization"—such as hoarding ill-gotten gains, exploiting the poor, and masking such evils under the garb of religion.

What has all this to do with preaching today? At first, apparently, not much. The first two chapters may yield only a few shining texts, such as one about "God's Love for the Poor" (2:6-7*a*). On the other hand, the opening part of the book sets forth the spirit of God's spokesman in the face of evils widespread and deep-seated, such evils as curse our large cities today. These chapters also help to make clear the remainder of the book. As for specific messages, they will come later, and in abundance.

Why not begin with "The Perils of Religious Privilege" (3:2)? Remember that Israel still professed to serve the God who had delivered the fathers from bondage. Instead of looking on Him as a tribal deity, or one of many, Israel referred to Him proudly as her only God. All of this sounds strangely like our own country. We have received from the Lord's hands more bountifully than any other people in history. What have we given Him in return? "Words, words, words!" Instead of looking on ourselves as His pets, we ought to know that when He gives a nation countless blessings, He expects loyalty in return. If like Israel we prove untrue, we ought to behold "the dark line in God's face."

The next sermon may call for still more courage. "What God Thinks of Our Houses." (3:15.) In every normal heart He has placed a love for home with its domestic joys. Ofttimes he moved the prophets to sound a call for piety

29

that centered in the home. But He also bade Amos rebuke anyone who erected a mansion by grinding the faces
of the poor. To this day He cannot sanction lavish display
and wanton luxury. In applying such truths a man needs
wisdom and tact from above. Still the message stands as a
danger signal.

THE SINS OF THE CHURCH (4:4–6:14)

The following section has to do with evils in the
church, rather than the state.[3] Such a distinction might not
have seemed clear to Amos or his hearers. In that time
church and state did not stand out so sharply in contrast
as with us today. Still we can make the distinction for our
own convenience. What Amos spoke about forms of
worship may now apply to the church. When he appeared
in Bethel, he found the state church popular and prosper-
ous, with elaborate forms devoid of righteousness. Hence
he spoke about "The Worship That God Hates." (5:21-
27.) Like the other prophets this one believed in worship,
both public and private, but never as a substitute for righteousness, the bedrock of all religion.

Again he launched out against "The Luxury That Defiles" (6:1-14). After an amazing picture of luxury made
possible through oppression, he foretold judgment soon to
fall at the Captivity. In vain he pleaded with the people

---

[3] See the monumental work by Anson P. Stokes, *Church and State in the
United States,* 3 vols. (New York: Harper & Bros., 1950).

THE VOICE OF GOD'S RIGHTEOUSNESS
THE PREACHER WHO FAILED (7:10-17)

The book as a whole includes some of the mightiest preaching in Holy Scripture. In almost every respect save continued optimism Amos showed power. As a master of style he displayed clarity, beauty, and force. If at times his words lacked elegance, he merely let the style accord with the substance. Drawing figures from the hill country he knew best, he spoke of sophisticated city folk as heifers in heat, rushing "out at the breach, every one straight before her." As a son of the soil he could see life without veneer, and then paint what he saw, with none of the glamour that starry-eyed idealists often cast over vice. Would that Amos might teach many a young minister today how to speak with force and with fire.

Even so, as a message from God, and not as a piece of art, this man's preaching seems to have failed. By strictures against the state he aroused the enmity of the rulers. By criticism of the church he incurred the hatred of both priests and false prophets. He did not even have an opportunity to complete that sermon. What a contrast to the record of many a pastor now, with popular acclaim and increasing security! On the other hand, how much of our pulpit work today will live on to bless the world as long as that of "unsuccessful Amos"?

When the priest of Bethel stopped the prophet in the midst of his discourse, the latter showed the sort of stuff out of which God makes a spokesman. This man preached

35

because he had a call from God. Unlike Balaam, and many another product of a "manufactured ministry," Amos spoke and wrote what the world will never let die. Without schooling, or what we call culture, this son of the soil has much to show about what it means to preach. Like Spurgeon or Moody, William Booth or Gipsy Smith, this earlier man proved that God does not rely exclusively on men from the schools of the prophets.

Among men of culture in the church of recent times John Kelman took a high rank. In Edinburgh he ministered to the elite, including many from the University of Edinburgh. Yet in his lectures at Yale he told what he had learned about preaching with authority. In contrast with his polished discourses an elderly layman, not educated, spoke about the sermons of an untutored evangelist in a meeting not far away: "In the tent they aye say 'You,' but when ye're preachin' ye say 'We.' "

"The shrewd judgment," said Kelman, "intended for approbation, led to a change in my use of personal pronouns for which I have often thanked the old friend of my young days." [5] Why did not the Scotsman learn that lesson from the prophet Amos? Courage to say "you"!

Alas, not every young minister knows how to read this book. In student days I plodded through it all, but could find only one bit that appealed to me. The prophet's words

[5] See *The War and Preaching* (New Haven: Yale University Press, 1919), p. 208.

36

"Prepare to meet thy God" (4:12c) suggested a little evangelistic talk—little in more ways than one. A year or two later A. B. Davidson, George Adam Smith, and A. F. Kirkpatrick taught me what should have seemed evident at a glance, that the prophet addressed these words to the nation. Today every congregation needs an interpreter to guide the layman in reading prophetic books intelligently and with practical helpfulness. Some of this guidance ought to come from the pulpit on the Lord's Day, and still more from the pastor's teaching hour later in the week. What a way to "put new life into the old prayer meeting"! [6]

Amos has a message for us all today, a message of which a few men in history have had too much of a monopoly. During the past 2,700 years conditions on the surface of the earth have changed many times, but righteousness and judgment, repentance and mercy, remain much the same as of old. Today through the local interpreter of truth and duty the Lord God would speak to our people here in the States:

"You only have I known of all the families of the earth. Therefore I will visit upon you all your iniquities." "Prepare to meet thy God, O America!"

[6] See my *Preaching from the Bible* (New York and Nashville: Abingdon-Cokesbury Press, 1941), ch. IX, "The Bible Reading."

CHAPTER III

Hosea

THE GOSPEL FROM A BROKEN HEART

SOME OF US LOVE THE BOOK OF HOSEA MORE THAN ANY other prophetic writing. Personally I owe much of this feeling to Sargent's frieze of the prophets in the public library at Boston. One summer as a student, before the prophets had begun to mean much to me, I used to stop each morning to study those historic figures. Later in the day, when leaving the library, I would pause again to bask in the presence of my new heroes. Soon two of them began to mean more than any of the others. On these two the artist seems to have done his most enduring work, both as an interpreter of the Bible and as a portrayer of human personality.

First of all stood out the robust manliness and vigor of Isaiah, who has become the hero of many a young minister. Gradually the figure of Hosea began to take a place equally prominent. With a face like that of the Lord Jesus and eyes that should have melted the hardest heart, this man of old showed that university student the meaning and glory of prophetic goodness. Clad in white, as a symbol of purity like that of snow fresh from the skies,

Hosea stands out today in many a copy of that frieze. What could better adorn the wall of a young pastor's study?

Ere long that frieze led me to a study of the prophetic books, if only to discover how nearly Sargent had caught the spirit of those ancient seers. While he seemed to have fallen short with other prophets, the artist's portrayal of Hosea accorded with the book from this man with a broken heart. Both the book and the artist made me think of Hosea as the most Christlike of all the seers, with the possible exception of Jeremiah. That study also disclosed, much to my dismay, that this little book of the Bible bristled with difficulties, most of which have not disappeared. Not to speak of critical issues that concern technical scholars, the book baffles practical teachers who depend largely on making outlines. Who can set forth the bony framework of a book that breathes out the sighs of a broken heart? Even so, this work has a message that concerns us all, for it deals with the problem of adultery. Better still, by far, Hosea discusses the issue in a spirit like that of the Cross. Note, as a witness, a British scholar who writes about this Gospel from a broken heart:

The Gospel of Hosea is that of a love able to transform life by creating a new attitude within, leading to a new interpretation of all things without, a new meaning. For spiritual beings, all that really matters is the meaning of things, and man's spirit is capable of any miracle of transformation, when

39

once aroused to its task. The great idea of love must be wrought out in life to become actual, and so effective. It was made actual first by the cross of Hosea; it culminated in the Cross of Christ, and it is continued in the countless other crosses of God's prophets and apostles in all generations.[1]

This man Hosea, with the cross in his heart, lived in the time of Isaiah. According to Sellin, a German scholar, Hosea prophesied about 750-725 B.C. Hosea belonged in the Northern Kingdom, whereas Isaiah lived in the Southern. Both of them faced the aftermath of what we know as "good times." Isaiah preached much about the nation as a whole, and about the surrounding powers of earth. The other man felt more concern about the homes of God's children, and about their hearts. Like his coming Lord and Redeemer, Hosea thought mainly in terms of one home and one heart, as typical of many.

THE TRAGEDY OF A BROKEN HOME

In Israel of old, as in our country now, broken homes appeared on every side. From some of them, following bad examples, young girls went out to serve as temple priestesses. As in India of late, young women sold their bodies within sacred walls, and men indulged in beastliness under the shadow of the sanctuary—all in the name of their gods. Then as now perversion of love into lust undermined the

---

[1] See H. Wheeler Robinson, *The Cross of Hosea* (London: Lutterworth Press; Philadelphia: Westminster Press, 1949), p. 64.

40

morals of men and women. Whatever the reason, bodily impurity opens the way for all sorts of degradation and filth. Disloyalty to God in the home leads to indecency in every walk of life. All of this appears in the early chapters of Hosea's book.

This prophet spoke out of his own experience of suffering. Like St. Augustine, Hosea knew impurity firsthand; but unlike the later man, the seer did not so sin himself. Why do impurity and its antithesis bulk large in Augustine's masterpieces, the *Confessions* and the *City of God?* Probably because they had loomed large in the early years of that future saint. In a sense the same held true of Hosea, but he had kept his hands clean and his heart pure. Today when impurity stalks our streets unashamed, putting out the fires on many a hearth, this man of God has a message for the church. He shows us how to deal with sex, and not by suggestion lead to still more vice. In the writings of this prophet the discussion of sex appears as pure as the snow on Mount Hermon.

The opening portion of the book tells about Gomer, a "prodigal wife." At some stage in her career she became an adulteress. As the wife of Hosea, Gomer stooped to sin with her body—not only once or twice, but again and again. At first she may have been swept off her feet by a sudden surge of temptation, but if so, ere long she sold herself to a life of sin. After a while she left her husband and three little ones, of whom he may not have been the father. All of this against a husband with a soul as white as snow! Did ever human nature stoop lower than that of Gomer?

From this point onward the tale does not run clearly, but a few facts stand out. Lower and lower Gomer seems to have sunk in sin, and that without shame. Little by little she must have lost her charms. At last when her paramour had sated his lust, he flung her aside as a thing of shame. In the course of time, like a common slave, she stood exposed for sale in the open market. There Hosea bought her at the price the law prescribed for a slave gored by a bull. Then he took her to his home, and here the tale ends, in as far as it has to do with the "prodigal wife." These basic facts appear in Holy Writ, with only enough surmises here to make them stand out boldly.

What do the facts mean? The answer must remain more or less uncertain. Surely no writer ought to seem dogmatic. The darkest problem has to do, not with Hosea and with Gomer, but with holiness and with God. At the beginning the book says that God commanded Hosea: "Go, take unto thee a wife of whoredom and children of whoredom, for the land doth commit great whoredom, departing from the Lord" (1:2). What a command from the God who takes delight in holiness! As such He appears in all the prophetic writings, and nowhere more than in those of Hosea. How could the Holy One command a saint to marry a woman he knew to be impure?

Before anyone dares to preach from the later portions of this book, he ought to make up his mind about this initial problem. In the works of scholars he will find three theories.

A few writers interpret the facts literally. They believe that the purest of saints married the foulest of women and lived with her for years, knowing that she had sinned with her body and had never shown sorrow. Apart from the problem about Hosea, this theory runs counter to all that the Bible teaches about God. Scholars who so interpret the facts seem to forget that Hosea had the soul of a poet. Except for sixteen verses of prose narrative the book consists of poetry. It appeals to imagination far more than reason, and calls for reading with the heart more than the brain.

Other scholars look on these passages as allegorical. So do many lay readers. A lifelong student of the Bible may never dream that Hosea, like St. Augustine, wrote out of facts in his own experience. Anyone who looks at the record with care can see that it purports to be a sober account of what occurred in the writer's home. If anyone looks on the record as allegorical because the facts do not accord with his ideas about God, he sets up a precedent that may lead him astray elsewhere in the Bible. How shall he regard other narrative portions of Holy Writ? As full of fact or of fiction?

Still another theory we may term the retrospective.

This view accords with much that we know about the Hebrew mind. Let us assume that when Hosea married Gomer he looked on her as pure. Little by little, then more and more, he began to suspect her faithfulness. He became so suspicious that he gave the second child a name reflecting his fears about his wife, and the third a name showing certainty about Gomer's sin. When at last she deserted both husband and children, Hosea learned truths he might never have known if he had not suffered from a broken heart. Looking back, before he wrote this book, he could see in all his career the guiding hand of God.

After Hosea had found his way out into the sunlight of God's truth, the Holy Spirit moved him to write this account of the tragedy in his home. At last he could see that God had been making all things work together for good. So much for the retrospective theory. For another example from Holy Writ, turn to the record about Joseph's forgiveness of his brethren. He too had suffered deadly wrongs at the hands of loved ones against whom he had not sinned. At last he became willing to forgive and seek reconciliation. Why? Because he had learned to look on all that tragedy as it related to the providence of God. "It was not you that sent me hither, but God." (Gen. 45:8a.) "Ye meant evil against me; but God meant it for good." (Gen. 50:20a.)

Let us assume the validity of the retrospective theory, and in its light review the facts about Gomer. Her course

44

downward may have begun gradually, perhaps impercep-
tibly. As a shy maiden at home she may never have
dreamed that she would ever stoop to folly. When she became the bride of Hosea, she may not yet have sold her
body to a seducer. She seems never to have known the
worth of saintly Hosea. How else could she have yielded
to the blandishments of an oversexed showman who lured
her from home, sated his lust, and then flung her aside as
a thing for "scorn to point her slow, unmoving finger at"?
To share the orgies of such a brute, who may have looked
as handsome as a bull, she broke up her home and deserted
her bairns just when they most needed a mother's love. So
much for this tragedy of a broken home.

The Tragedy of an Adulterous Church

Why did God permit such a saint as Hosea to suffer as
in a burning fiery furnace heated from the depths of hell?
Perhaps because the Lord wished him to sympathize with
many another in like distress. The prophet lived in a country full of broken homes and bleeding hearts. Looking
out over his own threshold he could see many another
household with mother or father worse than dead because
of adultery. The parallel with our own land today reminds
us of the need for sympathy with every innocent victim
of an adulterous mate. Unless the interpreter stands on
guard, he may forget to deal with the book in hand while
he launches out into other waters.

Gradually the prophet must have sensed a deeper truth. Not only should he show compassion for everyone whose marriage had gone on the rocks, but God's interpreter ought also to make clear that the people as a whole had committed adultery against the Holy One. At first the figure may startle, even appall. What weaker words, however, could set forth the enormity of a disloyal church? Like other seers of old, this one often spoke of God as the Husband of Israel. If pagan nations proved untrue, they committed fornication. They never had plighted their troth to the God of Israel. When His own people turned aside to sin with other gods, willfully and habitually, they indulged in adultery. Not even Hosea as a prophet inspired of God could have used a blacker word, more full of filth.

Why did the Church as the Bride of God prove untrue? He had set His love upon her, and had chosen her for priceless joys. He had never let her go or given her any excuse for wandering thoughts and wicked desires. Without reason the Church of God had forsaken her first love, and turned aside to other deities—most of all to Baal, the god of Syria next door. "She went after other gods and forgat me," said the Lord. She acted as though the good things of earth had come from Baal, and to him she sold herself in sin.

As in our own times, disloyalty to God showed itself in public worship. Like other prophets, Hosea believed in

46

corporate worship, but never as a substitute for loyalty to God. The prophet saw in the worship of his day a series of empty forms, without any movement of sinful hearts Godward. He saw people turning away from those hollow rites, with all their mockery and sham, to engage in the foul practices of surrounding peoples. He knew that all such disloyalty to God constituted a cancer gnawing at the vitals of the Church. What would the seer think of the worship in your home church today?

Hand in hand with sins of worship went offenses against decency. Private lives became more and more corrupt. Sins against society abounded. All this the prophet included under his charge of spiritual adultery. More than any other prophet except Jeremiah, this earlier seer beheld the inwardness of sin. He saw that "the inward attitude shows itself in the outward action." Back of all personal and social evils lay the lack of heart love for God. When one generation turned away from God, and went after Baal, the next generation suffered from the aftermath of disloyalty. When people sow the wind, their children reap the whirlwind. So the prophet kept protesting out of a heart broken by sorrows in his home.

The Wonders of Forgiving Grace

Largely through his own sufferings, and through sympathy with others in distress, the prophet must have caught a new vision of divine grace. "As we expand [Hosea's

47

message] in the light of the Incarnation, we dare to think of a love which embraces all mankind, an almighty love which will not be content until all things are subject unto it, *that God may be all in all*." [2] Hosea learned that God too could suffer, and still keep on loving those who had done Him the deadliest wrongs. In bringing about a reconciliation with His sinful people, the Lord took the initiative. In this course of love and mercy He persevered, so that Frederick W. Faber could sing:

> There's a wideness in God's mercy,
> Like the wideness of the sea.

To us these truths about God's love may sound like an "old, old story." Through countless hymns and sermons the good news has issued from the New Testament. In Hosea's day such words of love and mercy would have sounded strange. In his own heart they must have led to an unexpected decision. Just as Joseph's love for Father Jacob and for Jacob's God had led to the forgiveness of elder brethren who had done Joseph deadly wrongs, so the mercy of God to an erring people must have led Hosea to forgive adulterous Gomer. Why should we of today extend the olive branch? Because God for the sake of His dear Son forgives us, man by man.

This kind of love calls for action. When Hosea saw

[2] See A. F. Kirkpatrick, *The Doctrine of the Prophets* (London: Macmillan and Co., 3rd ed.), pp. 140-41.

his wife exposed for sale as a common slave, he bought her for his own, and took her to the home she had deserted. He never had ceased to love her, and his heart bade him treat her as Almighty God had dealt with His unfaithful Church. How Gomer responded to forgiving love, no one now can tell. At last she may have begun to see into the heart of the one whom she had wronged. As long as Gomer lived she may have striven to prove worthy of the one who had rescued her from the scrap heap and restored her to his hearth.

By way of illustration think of two contrasting scenes. Ask which of them more nearly shows the spirit of Hosea. In Tennyson's *Idylls of the King*, Arthur stands out as the noblest gentleman of that olden time. To Guinevere as queen he gives all his love and devotion. Later he finds her untrue, not only once or twice, but again and again. In sorrow he grants pardon, and then watches her hie away to a nunnery. In bidding her farewell after his forgiveness the King uses these words:

> All is past, the sin is sinn'd, and I,
> Lo, I forgive thee, as Eternal God
> Forgives!

At the nunnery she abides through years of penance and at last becomes the abbess. In a ripe old age, full of good works, she passes to where "beyond these voices there is peace."

The contrasting scene has to do with a young man and woman whom we shall call John and Mary. The facts come from the minister concerned, and appear in a form that cannot embarrass the two young folks. Mary and John had been engaged, but she had become infatuated with another man whom she had loved "not wisely but too well." One day John walked into the pastor's study and inquired if Mary had been admitted to the local Crittenton Home for unmarried mothers. The minister knew about Mary's admission, but hesitated to disclose the facts to a stranger. After he had listened to John's tale, the older man went out to the Home and arranged for the young folks to meet, with himself as the witness whom the rules required. There he sat with an aching heart, for he knew that Mary would soon bring forth a child.

As she entered the room her steps faltered. When she saw John coming forward to embrace her, Mary cried out: "No, John, you must forgive me, and then say good-by. We must never meet again." He would not have it so. He took her in his arms, told her that she had been more sinned against than sinning, that he had sought her in city after city, and he would never let her go as long as he lived. He wanted to marry her at once, and take her to his home. When she heard him speak about wedlock and a father's name for her unborn babe, she again burst into sobs, but at last she let her heart have its way and put herself forever into his loving care.

From the Board of the Home the minister secured permission to unite the two in marriage. Then he helped John rent a humble home and secure work on the streetcar line. In a few weeks the pastor learned that Mary had given birth to a little daughter. In after years he told a few of us about John's continued devotion to Mary and to the little girl. Then the minister's eyes filled with tears when he tried to tell about Mary's love for John. She loved much because she had received forgiveness like that of God the Father. Into the mouth of her husband, far more fitly than on the lips of King Arthur, Tennyson might have put the well-known words:

> I forgive thee, as Eternal God
> Forgives!

THE GOSPEL FROM A BROKEN HEART

Up to this point we have been thinking about the meaning of Hosea's experience. Now let us consider some of the preaching values. Among them all we can merely glance at one here and another there. After a lover of God and His Book enters into the spirit of this prophecy, he can return to it again and again, each time to discover a new facet of redeeming grace. Instead of wasting precious hours in a vain endeavor to compress these chapters into a symmetrical pattern, why not take the book as it stands? Let it speak from the heart of the writer to that of the interpreter. Then gradually you will begin to hear three verbs, each of them active, which ring out from the Gospel According to Hosea. From the verses that appear below, you can preach three sorts of sermons about God's redeeming grace.

THE IMPORTANCE OF RELIGIOUS KNOWLEDGE

First of all, hear the word "know." Know the Lord! All through this little book sounds the clarion call to know. As with Luther and others at the Reformation, Hosea calls for intelligent religion. If Israel had sensed the goodness of God, if Gomer had known the heart of her husband, if Mary had understood the depth of John's love, such knowledge would have set up a barrier against sin. From this point of view one can find in the book of Hosea more than a few golden words about "The Psychology of Sin." Let us follow this trail for a while, and translate into terms of today what we read on each guidepost. Through Hosea we can hear God speaking to us now.

"[Israel] did not know that I gave her the grain, and the new wine, and the oil, and multiplied unto her silver and gold, which they made into the image of Baal." (2:8 margin.) What ingratitude to God! Topic of the sermon, "America's Favorite Sin." Like Israel, our land has received from God's bounty all she has used in homage to man-made substitutes for God. In comparison with the blessings Israel enjoyed, our own mercies seem stupendous.

Hence our ingratitude seems all the more ghastly. Why do we not show gratitude to God? According to Hosea, the root sin lies in ignorance. Many of us do not recognize God as our Supreme Benefactor. When shall we repent for our ingratitude to the Giver of all, and begin acting as stewards of His bounty?

"The Lord hath a controversy with the inhabitants of the land, because there is no truth, nor goodness, nor knowledge of God in the land." (4:1.) "What God Thinks of Our Country." "My people are destroyed for lack of knowledge." (4:6a.) "The Perils of Religious Illiteracy." What did our chaplains find among soldiers, sailors, and airmen during the war? Appalling ignorance of the A B C in religion. Partly for this reason many a young warrior fell victim to all sorts of vice. "Whoredom and wine and new wine take away the understanding." (4:11.) "The Worst Thing About Vice." Not only does ignorance lead to sin; sin fosters ignorance. Here emerges what the scholars term "the noetic effects of sin." None but the pure in heart can see God, and really know Him. Sin has a way of blinding the eyes of a man who persists in doing wrong. Like Samson blind in Gaza the victim of evil may not know that God has departed from him, and has left him bound in chains.

Fortunately, the book of Hosea points to "a door of hope" which has to do with knowing God. "I will even betroth thee unto me in faithfulness; and thou shalt know

53

the Lord." (2:20.) These promises full of hope relate to the people collectively, and tell about "The Illumination of Divine Love." When once people get right with God, they find that the sunshine of His love guides them into richer and fuller understanding. At first they may not comprehend much about His ways, but as members of His redeemed family they keep on growing, both in grace and in knowledge.

"Let us know, let us follow on to know the Lord: his going forth is as sure as the morning; and he will come to us as the rain, as the latter rain that watereth the earth." (6:3.) "The Joys of Discovering God." When the prophet thinks about the joys of such a quest, he bursts into song. Here he says that whenever we start out to discover God, we meet Him along the way. In fact we find that He has been seeking us with gentleness like the shining of the morning sun on the western hills, and quietness like the falling of rain on a new-mown meadow. So the Spirit of God comes to refresh souls that long for His presence and benediction:

> How silently, how silently,
>   The wondrous gift is given!
> So God imparts to human hearts,
>   The blessings of His heaven.

"I desire goodness and not sacrifice; and the knowledge of God more than burnt-offerings." (6:6.) "The Spirit of

Our Worship." In Hosea's day many churchgoers thought of public worship as a sort of magic. They looked on automatic performance of certain rites as a guarantee of God's favor and blessing. From this prophet they learned that ceremonies meant little or much according to the spirit of those who rendered sacrifices to God. Better no worship at all than the sort of magic that does not enlist the heart. Now that churches of many kinds have begun to experience a "liturgical revival," the warning from God through Hosea ought to sound forth. Worship as a means of grace, but never as an end in itself.

These passages about the importance of religious knowledge lead up to the call for "A New Pilgrim's Progress." "Who is wise, that he may understand these things? prudent, that he may know them? for the ways of the Lord are right, and the just shall walk in them; but transgressors shall fall therein." (14:9.) The way to God seems to begin with knowing Him aright, and that in turn calls for the preaching of doctrine from the Bible. When the friend in the pew begins to understand God, he ought to start out on a pilgrimage of faith. The teaching here in Hosea resembles that in the Fourth Gospel, "This is life eternal, that they should know thee the only true God, and him whom thou didst send, even Jesus Christ" (17:3).[3]

In Hosea, as in the Fourth Gospel, knowledge includes

[3] See also Deut. 6:4-9. Like Hosea and John, Deuteronomy stresses both knowledge and love. Three of the best books in the Bible!

far more than information. To know God means to understand Him with both heart and brain. Some of us need to think with Phillips Brooks about "The Mind's Love of God." "No man completely and worthily loves any noble thing or person unless he loves with his mind as well as with heart and soul." Himself a foursquare personality, Brooks called for "thoughtful saints, men and women earnest, lofty, spiritual, but also full of intelligence, knowing the meaning and the reason of the things they believe, and not content to worship the God to whom they owe everything, with less than their whole nature." [4]

The Supremacy of Love to God

From the importance of knowing God we now turn to a far more vital matter, that of loving Him. Often in Hosea the two words—"know" and "love"—appear together and in this order. In passage after passage Hosea tells how knowledge of God leads to love for Him. As a rule the stress on knowing Him appears in the first half of the book, and that on love for Him in the latter part. Even where the word "love" does not appear, the idea permeates the book as the salt saturates the sea. The prophet would have agreed with Henry Drummond's essay about love as *The Greatest Thing in the World*, and with a stronger man, Jonathan Edwards, in his *Treatise*

[4] See *Sermons Preached in English Churches* (New York: E. P. Dutton and Co., 1910), pp. 24, 41.

56

Concerning Religious Affections. There the stalwart philosopher makes clear that our relations with God have far more to do with feelings than with thoughts. In our religion, as all through life,

> His heart was in his work,
>   and the heart
> Giveth grace unto every art. . . .
> Ah, how skillful grows the hand
> That obeyeth love's command!
>
> It is the heart and not the brain
> That to the highest doth attain.[5]

In the book of Hosea love often points to God's love for us, rather than our love for Him. According to this Gospel in the Old Testament we mortals need most of all to love God, and we can do that most surely after we discover how He first loved us. Thus the prophet anticipates the Beloved Disciple: "Herein is love, not that we loved God, but that he loved us, and sent his Son to be the propitiation for our sins" (I John 4:10). Along this upward trail of discovery the prophet went as far as anyone could journey before the Lord Christ came to reveal the love of God in person, supremely on the Cross. Since Hosea caught the feeling of Calvary, let us turn to some of his words about "love divine, all loves excelling."

[5] Longfellow, "The Building of the Ship."

"I will betroth thee unto me for ever; yea, I will betroth thee unto me in righteousness, and in justice, and in lovingkindness, and in mercies." (2:19.) "The Love of God for His Church." What higher honor could the Lord of creation bestow upon the Church than to choose her as His bride? If anyone wishes to interpret such prophetic words, he must cherish a lofty ideal of marriage, and also of the Church as the Bride of God (see Isa. 62:1-5; Eph. 5:25-27; *et al.*).

Under a different figure the prophet sings about "The Love That Adopts Children." "I will have mercy upon her that had not obtained mercy; and I will say to them that were not my people, Thou art my people; and they shall say, Thou art my God." (2:23*bc*.) Only the waif or changeling who has existed in an orphans' home, and then has received a welcome into a Christian family, can begin to sense the warmth and the glow that attend this idea of God's adopting sons and daughters. What a priceless message for today, when hosts of displaced persons all about us exist like abandoned children in a world where the Lord yearns to adopt them into the household of the redeemed!

Not all love, as we often use the word, deserves honorable mention in Holy Writ. In the heart of his book our prophet declares that God's people "consecrated themselves unto the shameful thing, and became abominable like that which they loved" (9:10). "The Love That Defiles." Think about the perversion of love in

Hosea's "prodigal wife," over against the sacrificial devotion of Susanna Wesley, the mother of John and Charles. In the Scriptures, Gomer stands for lust, rather than love. Lust consists in prostituting the most godlike powers of the human personality. The experience of Gomer in receiving forgiveness from Hosea enables us to see the door of hope for the worst of sinners.

Here also shines out "The Love That Nurtures." "When Israel was a child, then I loved him, and called my son out of Egypt. . . . I taught Ephraim to walk; I took them on my arms; but they knew not that I healed them." (11:1, 3.) Once again the prophet appeals to imagination. Anticipating the teachings of the New Testament about God, Hosea shows the lovingkindness of the Father in the nurture of His redeemed children. In the New Testament such passages usually refer to God's children one by one, but in Hosea's book the love of the Father relates to the people as a whole.

Rightly did the Lord often address those people as "children of Israel." Sometimes He looked on them with favor as resembling little children, and again with disappointment because they seemed childish. Still He loved them and taught them to take the first few faltering steps in the way of His commandments. He watched over them tenderly, and when they fell, He lifted them up to walk by holding His hand. "Like as a father pitieth his children, so the Lord pitieth them that fear him." (Ps. 103:13.)

While this truth of God's fatherhood through redemption stands out more boldly in the New Testament, the teaching also appears in the Old, and not least in the Gospel According to Hosea.

> The heart of the Eternal
> Is most wonderfully kind.

"How shall I give thee up, Ephraim? how shall I cast thee off, Israel? . . . My heart is turned within me, my compassions are kindled together. I will not execute the fierceness of mine anger, I will not return to destroy Ephraim: for I am God, and not man; the Holy One in the midst of thee; and I will not come in wrath." (11:8-9.) "The Love That Perseveres." "O Love that wilt not let me go." Among our countless reasons for gratitude, do we often thank God for His patience and His unwillingness to let us go on in the broad way of the world? Instead of dealing with such a truth abstractly, or else pontifically, why not relate it to the prophet's love for Gomer?

These passages in Hosea about the love of God keep growing better and better. They come to a climax in the closing chapter. "I will heal their backsliding, I will love them freely; for mine anger is turned away." (14:4.) "The Love That Transforms." Through Hosea the Lord God makes known the wonder of His redeeming work. He loves us with an everlasting love. He waits to heal the Church that has suffered through backsliding. He not only forgives all her waywardness and takes away the stains of her sin. He also transforms the weak and helpless into the strong and saintly. What a Gospel and what a God!

Thus far we have been thinking about two verbs, each of them active. Know! Love! The first has to do chiefly with us and our discovery of God; the second largely concerns Him and His goodness in making Himself known. Now we come to still another verb, which calls for action. "Turn!" In the Hebrew form this term means much the same as our word "conversion," with something of what we call repentance. "Turn!" "About Face!" "March!" "On to the City of God!" The Lord calls for action in the light of our knowledge about Him, and in response to His love for us. These passages in Hosea may lead to a series of evangelistic messages under the following heading.

THE BIBLE MEANING OF CONVERSION

"Their doings will not suffer them to turn unto their God; for the spirit of whoredom is within them, and they know not the Lord." (5:4.) "The Chief Barrier to Conversion." Many people all about us do not have the "will to believe." By deliberate choice of evil they block the way to reconciliation with God. In pointing out this barrier the prophet does not mean to discourage evildoers, but rather to stress the difficulty of breaking away from an ungodly past. Hosea makes clear that anyone who so desires can find a way to escape from bondage. Let him fall down on his knees and confess his sins. If he does this sincerely and in sorrow, he will find a way out into the sunlight and peace of forgiveness and cleansing.

"I will go and return to my place, till they acknowledge their offence, and seek my face: in their affliction they will seek me earnestly." (5:15.) "The Lord's Desire for Conversions Today." What patience on the part of our God! He knows how to wait in holy expectation. On the human level this truth stands out in the dealings of Hosea with Gomer. Just as his heart went forth to his "prodigal wife" with a love that never would let her go, the Lord God longs for the return of His prodigal Church. The same Father heart yearns for the return of everyone who has journeyed into the far country and reveled in the delights of sin. According to Dr. Fulton J. Sheen ten million men and women of this kind roam our streets and rural lanes looking for a way to escape from the far country. Would that every one of them might turn to God as He appears in the Gospel According to Hosea!

"Come and let us return unto the Lord; for he hath torn, and he will heal us; he hath smitten, and he will bind us up. After two days will he revive us: on the third day he will raise us up, and we shall live before him. (6:1-2.) "The Pathway to a Revival." This kind of religious awakening and renewal can come only from God. He alone can revive and restore. He chooses to do so in part through those who come to Him as penitents, throwing themselves on

His mercy. Who but He can bind up the broken heart and heal the ravaged soul? In such a spirit of dependence on redeeming love the noblest of our evangelistic hymns leads a lone penitent to sing:

> Just as I am, poor, wretched, blind;
> Sight, riches, healing of the mind—
> Yea, all I need, in Thee to find,
>   O Lamb of God, I come.

"Sow to yourselves in righteousness, reap according to kindness; break up your fallow ground; for it is time to seek the Lord, till he come and rain righteousness upon you." (10:12.) "The Gospel from the Old Home Farm." As a lover of the open country Hosea sings about the gospel in terms of seedtime and harvest. He assumes that the children of God desire to bring forth in abundance "the fruit of the Spirit," and he pleads with them to prepare for a large ingathering. Instead of sowing iniquity, or letting fields grow wild until they become infested with weeds, he bids God's husbandmen make ready for a harvest pleasing to the Owner of all. The Lord in turn stands ready to bless the work of their hands, just as He causes rain to fall on the wheat as it ripens toward the harvest.

Would that our country might experience such a revival! No one born since the outbreak of World War I has witnessed a widespread revival of religion according to the ideals of Holy Scripture. For an example of such a religious awakening look back to the days of Dwight L. Moody, especially in Great Britain; of John Wesley and his brother Charles; and of Martin Luther, with other reformers.[6] Better still, go back to the Day of Pentecost, and to the Old Testament, which on many a page tells about declension and renewal. Thus you will see, every time in a different fashion, much the same experiences for which Hosea pleads. Know the Lord, receive the love of God, and turn unto Him. Instead of stressing these truths one at a time, as we have been doing, Hosea sounds a gospel that calls for the three together, as we can find them now in the Cross. Know the Lord! Love Him! Turn to Him!

The young minister can become a biblical evangelist with a heart like that of Hosea. Like George W. Truett or Charles H. Spurgeon, let the spirit of the gospel permeate all your messages from the pulpit. In order to preach this way, live with Hosea until you share his passion for the return of the weak and the erring, one by one. Then by the grace of God you can help to bring about a revival in the home community, and it may be far beyond.

In all such preaching of the evangel the intellect should have its place. Like Hosea, learn to love God with your mind. Better still, let the love of God take control of your heart and your lips. Then plead with men and women, one by one, until they turn to God for pardon, cleansing,

---

[6] See James Burns, *Revivals: Their Laws and Leaders* (London: Hodder and Stoughton, 1909).

and peace. As G. Campbell Morgan used to insist, no man preaches well unless he moves the will of the hearer Godward. Partly by appealing to the reason, more by speaking to the heart, move the entire personality of the hearer to reach out and lay hold of redeeming grace. When you bring the unsaved or unchurched hearer to "the cross of Hosea" and to the Cross of his Lord, you can watch the penitent as he lays down the burden of sin and shame to receive the joy that the world cannot give or take away. Thank God for the Gospel According to Hosea!

CHAPTER IV

Micah

THE SPOKESMAN FOR THE COMMON PEOPLE

MICAH SPOKE FOR GOD ON BEHALF OF THE COMMON people. He arose in the latter part of the eighth century before Christ. Micah dwelt in the Southern Kingdom, not far southwest of where our Redeemer was born. This prophet lived under much the same sort of conditions as Amos and Hosea, his contemporaries. A half century of peace had brought temporal prosperity, but the prophet could see storms in the distance. To turn those storms aside, or guide his people through them, Micah spoke out boldly on behalf of the common folk. To them he belonged, by birth and by choice. For them he demanded justice, and with them he pleaded for loyalty to God.

This prophet has become known mainly in connection with Isaiah, the most admired of the Hebrew seers. The two men lived and spoke at about the same time, and said many of the same things, especially about world peace. They stand out more by way of contrast. Micah lived in the country, where he seems not to have known wealth or ease. Isaiah, a city man, appears to have been reared as a child of fortune. The rural prophet confined his gaze largely to Judah and Israel, especially Judah. The city orator looked out over the world of his day and spoke about the destinies of nations. Micah contented himself with messages to people of his own kind. Isaiah could speak to kings and make them tremble. The former, even when he soared, flew on a lower wing. The latter spoke and wrote as one of the world's foremost orators. In view of such contrasts, which one do you resemble—the prophet to the common people, or the most brilliant of the seers?

The Prophecy of Micah

The first chapter of Micah serves as the introduction. Here he pours out burning words about the sins of Judah. Also he voices grief that the people should require such a message. Here speaks the true prophet of God: plain teachings about sin and judgment, always with sadness of heart, and sometimes with tears. Even when he rebukes her shortcomings and failures, Micah shows that he cares for the motherland, and wishes her to enjoy the favor of God. Would that every parish had such a loving and faithful pastor!

The opening chapter no doubt seemed clear and interesting to people in Micah's day. It brings difficulty to us, because we do not see the local color. Still it shows how to begin a sermon. This one starts with the hearers where they are, at home in Judah. The opening words bring them into the presence of God, and prepare them for what His messenger has to say. Such an introduction quickens the hearer's imagination, but does not anticipate what will come later. As for preaching values today, they come after the opening chapter of Micah.

The body of the work falls into three main parts. The first has to do with the burdens and wrongs of the common people; the second, with the promise of better days to come; the third, with the religion God expects from the average man. The spirit of the book may become clear through an example from American history. In 1829 Andrew Jackson of Tennessee became the seventh President of the United States. In the White House for eight years he stood out as the friend and champion of the common people. Partly for this reason he became known in certain quarters as "a rough frontiersman, having few or none of the social graces."

On the contrary, says Henry Watterson, peerless editor of his day, Jackson personally was "a gentleman, a leader, a knight-errant, who captivated women and dominated men." The editor cites the testimony of two visitors from England, highly cultured, each of whom paid Jackson almost the same tribute: "The finest gentleman I ever met." [1] Over against this background put his words in vetoing a certain bill. Nowhere has a man in high office

[1] See Henry Watterson, *Marse Henry, An Autobiography* (New York: Doran, 1919) I, 33-35.

stated more clearly and strongly the principles that undergird the prophecy of Micah. The merits of the bill do not concern us now, but only the spirit of the President in contending for the rights of those who have to toil with their hands:

> The rich and powerful too often bend the acts of government to their own selfish purposes. Distinctions in society will appear under every just government. Equality of talents, of education, of wealth cannot be produced by human institutions. In the full enjoyment of the gifts of heaven and the fruits of superior industry, economy, and virtue, every man is equally entitled to protection by law. But when the laws undertake to add to those natural and just advantages artificial distinctions, to make the rich richer, and the potent more powerful, the humble members of society—the farmers, mechanics, and laborers—who have neither the time nor the means of securing like favors to themselves, have a right to complain of the injustices of their government.[2]

Where could anyone find a more accurate commentary on the first part of Micah's prophecy? According to the leading historical writer about the age of Jackson, in the year after he became President "five sixths of the persons in the jails of New England were debtors, most of them owing less than twenty dollars." Six years later a well-known religious writer declared: "No man can be obedient to God's will as revealed in the Bible without becoming

[2] See Arthur M. Schlesinger, Jr., *The Age of Jackson* (Boston: Little, Brown and Co., 1945), p. 95.

wealthy." [3] The devotees of such doctrines felt the strictures of Jackson like scourges. As professed lovers of the Bible little did they dream that the President unknowingly echoed and re-echoed the demands of Micah, the prophet of the common people.

THE GRIEVANCES OF THE COMMON PEOPLE (CHS. 2–3)

In the second and third chapters, Micah gives a bill of particulars. He shows the will of God concerning the idle rich and their oppression of the poor. Like the Master Himself, the prophet has no quarrel with wealth as such. Still he can see that many have succumbed to the peril of loving money. He insists that the worst citizens often appear, not so much among the poor, who have everything to drag them down, as among the rich, who have everything to lift them up. No doubt he could find wicked men among the poor and saints among the rich, but he saw a larger proportion of bad men among the idle rich.

The sins of these men had to do with the land. They may not have broken the laws of their country, which tended to favor men of might. Long years without war had brought increase of trade, which had led to swollen fortunes. Where could the rich invest their gains more securely than in farm lands? Hence the soil, the source of national well-being, came more and more into the hands of the favored few. The new owners may have committed

[3] *Ibid.,* pp. 129, 134.

no crime against the nation, but in the eyes of this prophet
they had broken the laws of God.

In order to get and keep these lands, the rich men needed
protection from politicians. Even the king on the throne
seems to have felt helpless in the hands of his noblemen.
These politicians accepted bribes from the idle rich, and
then joined with them in debauchery. In the eyes of the
prophet both classes indulged in cannibal feasts with the
poor as victims. In the sight of the Lord barbarous folk
who slay their foes and then devour human flesh do not
exceed in guilt the so-called upper classes who indulge in
orgies made possible by stealing land from the suffering
poor.

In Micah's day the oppressors also included leaders of
the Church. So he denounced the trinity of evildoers: idle
rich, corrupt politicians, and false prophets with unworthy
priests. Among the three groups he counted religious
leaders the worst. Living on the bounty of the rich,
basking in the favor of political rulers, such prophets found
it easy to justify the wicked for a reward. They knew how
to curry favor with men in high places, and how to bolster
up an unspeakable cause by pronouncing on it the blessing
of God. This sounds like Germany in days before Luther,
and like Spain in recent times.

The prophet cried out against this prostitution of men's
powers. As one of the common people he himself must
have suffered at the hands of the unholy triumvirate. In

71

any case he pronounced the judgment of God on the trinity of evildoers who conspired to defraud the poor. From that day until now holy men such as Micah have pleaded for the rights of the common people. Often their messages have related to distribution of the land. With political questions as such, spokesmen for God have no right to interfere. But when laws and customs make it hard for a workingman to support his family in comfort, the prophet of God dare not sit dumb. He must insist that no oppressor of the poor can escape the judgment of God.

The student of history need not look far for examples of such oppression. In the ancient world he can find them on every hand, and during certain periods little else. Why should he also discover such conditions in "Christian" lands? Think of France before her revolution, Russia prior to her upheaval, Mexico under Diaz, and Spain under Franco. The same old triumvirate of evil: the idle rich, the politicians, the false prophets or unholy priests—all conspiring against those whom they should have befriended. Sometimes the same combination works nearer home!

In view of such facts what should a minister of the gospel do today? Should he cease proclaiming the good news of salvation and become an advocate of social reform? The Lord forbid! Neither should he close his eyes to conditions in the world about him. As an interpreter of God's written Word let him give due place to such a prophecy as this from Micah. If some lay hearers protest, as a few of them will, he may reply that they should blame the Book and not the interpreter.

Years ago I went to lecture about the prophets at the leading conference of the Presbyterian Church in the U. S. Knowing that the denomination did not look with favor on preaching about politics, I asked the friend in charge what course to pursue in dealing with Micah and Amos. At once this leader replied: "Tell us anything you wish, provided you get it from the Bible, and show what it means today. We who live in the Bible Belt want you to declare the whole counsel of God." This was to me the first of many evidences that the dread of such teachings usually springs from the heart of the preacher, not from the friends in the pew. However much the truth may hurt, many of them want to know what the Bible says, and what it means today. They would like more of a popular teaching ministry, based on the Bible.[4]

In this kind of pulpit work an expositor need not confine himself to the Old Testament. In the closing scenes of our Lord's earthly life, as they appear in the Passion play at Oberammergau, the spectator can see much the same three groups of "willful men" as in the book of Micah. Who conspired to hound Christ to His Cross? Rich men who ground down the faces of the poor, rulers who administered laws in favor of the rich, and church leaders

[4] See Murray H. Leiffer, *The Layman Looks at the Minister* (New York and Nashville: Abingdon-Cokesbury Press, 1947), p. 50.

who invoked the blessing of God on oppressors of the poor. All this the Redeemer endured because He chose to serve among those who toiled with their hands. Herein lay no small part of what He suffered for us men and our salvation. Who follows in His train?

THE PROMISE OF BETTER DAYS (CHS. 4–5)

The next two chapters contain more of the good news that we associate with the New Testament. The prophet now turns his eyes toward the future and paints a word picture of earth in the golden age when the Lord shall have His way among men. Needless to say, these promises yet await fulfillment. Meanwhile they set up ideals that the minister ought to share with his lay friends, especially—

> Those beneath life's crushing load,
>   Whose forms are bending low,
> Who toil along the climbing way
>   With painful steps and slow.

One of these golden passages has to do with world peace as it relates to the farmer who toils with his hands (4:1-5). Much the same words appear in Isaiah (2:2-4), but with a difference. The better-known seer paints a wondrous picture of nations beating their swords into plowshares, but he shows nothing about the bearing on the ordinary man. Micah alone tells how the coming of peace on earth will

74

affect the person who suffers most from the ravages of war and who profits most from good will among the nations, the "forgotten man" of Micah's day and of our own.

This vision from God tells of a time when the nations will settle their disputes without resorting to strife. In our own early history when two men of passion had a quarrel they would settle their differences by a duel. Through a duel Aaron Burr took the life of Alexander Hamilton. In that same year, 1804, a minister named Eliphalet Nott preached a sermon about the sin and folly of dueling. Partly because of that message, dueling disappeared from the American scene. War still rages, and why? Partly because we who believe in the Book have not led "Christian nations" to apply its teachings about war and peace.

The prophet of the common people insists that war shall cease. The powers of earth ought to use in the arts of peace the resources they worse than waste in battles by land and sea and air. Think how we have squandered the flower of young manhood and the bounties of God's "good earth." Why not use all these resources in making our world more fair, a better dwelling place for God's little boys and girls? No wonder the vision of Micah reaches its climax in telling about the farmer under his own vine and fig tree, enjoying the fruits of work with his hands! In the cool of the evening, with little boys and girls playing about his knees, the farmer can thank God that "peace hath her victories no less renowned than war."

In that golden age we shall cease training our sons for war. We shall always need a police force, with men of training and skill, but we shall use them to maintain the peace. For almost 150 years, ever since the close of a needless war,[5] we have had peace on our northern border, the longest boundary line in the world. Why have we not gone to war with Canada by land or sea or air? Because after 1814 the two peoples agreed that they would prepare for peace, not war. They would station along that boundary line not a single soldier, and put on the Great Lakes not a single man-of-war. Hence the vision of Micah has become a fact of history.

How would the prophet extend such blessings over all the earth? Like the minister today, this spokesman for common people does not enter into details of world politics and international agreements. Rather does he show that the hope for world peace rests with God. He alone can remove the causes of war, such as hatred and fear, greed and race prejudice. Only the Almighty can change the hearts of men and nations. He chooses to do so by such old-fashioned methods as preaching, teaching, and living in love. From this point of view read and study the golden vision of Micah. Note that the coming of world peace, under God, depends mainly on the Church.

[5] I do not look on all our past wars as needless.

preme sacrifice? Like Abraham on Mount Moriah shall I make ready to offer up my first-born son?" No, the Lord will have none of that, save as He wishes parents to give a son or daughter for the ministry or the mission field. Even such a gift does not constitute the heart and glory of a man's religion. That calls for more than giving of things and of a loved one. Give yourself!

Micah believed in sacrifices and burnt offerings, much as we believe in forms of worship today, but only as means of grace. He looked forward to a time when the people of God would no longer need to offer animal sacrifices. Meanwhile he ministered to a childlike folk who required such ways of expressing devotion to God. Instead of that he found them making their offerings as substitutes for religion of the heart. So he gathered up the truth in words that everyone ought to know and ponder: "He hath showed thee, O man, what is good; and what doth the Lord require of thee, but to do justly, and to love kindness, and to walk humbly with thy God?" (6:8.)

In this golden verse three qualities stand out. So large do they bulk in the prophet's eye that they occupy most of the remaining paragraphs in his book. First of all, as the foundation of a man's religion, stands righteousness. This means being right with God, right with others, right with self. In view of such a basic requirement any man ought to hesitate. "Can I meet that requirement? No, not unless I receive a power mightier than my own. I need God to make me righteous. In terms of the New Testament, I need Christ and His Cross."

The second requirement calls for something more important, something harder to attain. Not only must a man do all that perfect righteousness demands, but he must also love kindness. If being right serves as the foundation of the house, lovingkindness affords the atmosphere of the home where the spirit of a man dwells. Like the prophet himself, a man ought to do right, even though that means a cross. While doing so he ought to look on kindness as far more like God. To qualify for admission to the family of the redeemed a man needs righteousness; to live in the family circle as one who belongs there he must have lovingkindness.

The third element may seem anticlimactic. At least it comes as a surprise. Do right, love kindness, and walk humbly with thy God. Good, better, best! In all history what other religion has ever stressed humility as the crowning virtue of the believer? In early manhood one may think of religion mainly in terms of doing right. Gradually one learns to appraise all such deeds according to the spirit that prompts them. "It's not doing that counts most," said a saintly missionary, "but being." In later years he would go one stage farther: "Not doing, or even being, but becoming!" When a man looks at his life as it must appear in the eyes of God, he becomes humble. The crowning virtue!

Every virtue we possess,
  And every victory won,
And every thought of holiness,
  Are His alone.

In making a study of this golden text in Micah, single out the nouns, or the equivalent of nouns: righteousness, kindness, and humility. Then stress the verbs, each of them active: to do, to love, and to walk. The last verb speaks of a man's religion as a *Pilgrim's Progress*. Walk with God! That calls for a life of deepening friendship with Him. To walk with God means to know Him so well and love Him so much that you count it life's utmost joy to live in His presence. To walk also means progress, or growth in humility. Once again, who can qualify?

These three requirements dominate the latter part of the book. Like every other teaching minister, this prophet understands the value of meaningful repetition. He also knows that anyone who would live according to this standard must rely upon his God. Hence the book closes with an apostrophe: "Who is a God like unto thee, that pardoneth iniquity, and passeth over the transgression of the remnant of his heritage?" (7:18a.)

The book of Micah opens with a call on the nation to behold her God as coming in a storm. The prophecy closes with a tender appeal to behold the same God in terms of love and forgiveness. Which of the two passages more fitly portrays the God with whom we have to do?

The One who stands for righteousness and judgment, or the One who delights in mercy and redeeming love? Like his coming Lord, the prophet revealed Him in both aspects, but most of all as the God of mercy and grace.

THE MESSAGE FOR THE PASTOR

If any young minister wishes to strengthen his own spiritual life, and also help the people grow in grace, let him live for three months with the book of Micah. Some parts he may not appreciate for a while. These he can master in time if he gets to know the background in history and the tone color of the prophetic writing. Even if some passages never yielded materials for sermons, he could select other portions full of light and warmth. He should learn to deal with any such truth personally, and not abstractly. To preach from any part of this book abstractly would mean to misrepresent the prophet of the common people. Whenever he wrote or spoke, Micah saw faces.

This little book should make a double appeal to the minister of a small church or one of average size. We think too much in terms of the stately edifice on Fifth Avenue and too little about the wayside chapel at Cream Ridge. We forget that Christianity was "born and bred in a brier patch." Why should the pastor and people in a small congregation develop an inferiority complex? "Oh, if we only had the numbers, equipment, and prestige of that church on Broadway!" My dear brother, "Thou shalt not covet thy neighbor's house," or his "field"!

From which sort of congregation does the Church at large draw the majority of her ministers and missionaries? Here and there a large city church, such as one in Hollywood, California, sends an unfailing stream of recruits into full-time Christian service. As a rule, however, the small rural congregation prepares a much larger proportion of sons and daughters for the work of the King at home and abroad. Where you find one divinity student with a background like that of young Isaiah, you can see a score with experiences like that of young Micah. For this reason, if for no other, we ought to foster small rural churches. If we let the springs run dry on the mountains, ere long we shall see the waters get low in the city reservoirs. What a parable for the small church and its minister!

The example of Micah encourages the pastor to concern himself with large issues. In the early years of a future Methodist bishop, a friend warned him: "You are contenting yourself with small themes. Why do you not study the great fundamentals of Christianity, and make them the staple of your ministry?" From that time onward young Candler started to "travel the great trunk lines of truth and became noted for his mastery of the major doctrines of the gospel." [6] From Micah he could have learned

[6] See Alfred M. Pierce, *Giant Against the Sky* (New York and Nashville: Abingdon-Cokesbury Press, 1948), p. 44.

how to stress the meaning of a man's religion, the spiritual bases of world peace, the rights of the farmer who toils with his hands, and other issues that concern every church-goer today.

From Micah a pastor can also learn to think and speak often in terms of a single hearer. The preacher may have in view an issue as broad as world peace or world brother-hood. Even so, he can make clear how it relates to a farmer sitting under the shade of an apple tree while he thinks about the future of his oldest son or daughter. From this point of view read again the prophecy of Micah. Then turn to the parables of our Lord. In every parable the Master deals with a vast truth or a commanding duty, but never apart from a person or two like the friend yonder in the back seat. For instance, take His parable about the growth of the Kingdom, or the one about the peril of riches. Hear Him speak about the farmer sowing his seed, and the rich man building his barn. What an appeal to the imagination of the friend in the pew!

Give a large place to the average man. Neither Micah nor his Lord would encourage a minister in putting any man first. Give the supreme place to God. With that pro-viso, pay much heed to the two-talent man, and the one-talent man. In the pulpit we keep talking in terms of the ten-talent man, both in the Scriptures and in life today. Either we discourage the average hearer, or else we give him a convenient alibi. In common with Micah and his

Lord, preach much about God in the experience of the ordinary man.

Also learn to esteem the one who toils with his hands. In many a rural community the church has not attracted and enlisted the tenant farmer, the share cropper, and the cotton mill worker. Almost without exception these men and their wives honor the name of Jesus. Do they also revere the local church and its pastor? They might do so if he saturated his soul with the spirit of Micah and then preached the gospel as it concerns the friend who toils with his hands—it may be on a slope like the one east of Bethlehem.

To preach like this old-time prophet requires courage. To rebuke men in high places, to demand fair dealings for those who toil on the farm—this may call for a spirit like that of Micah. Such pulpit work likewise calls for use of imagination. It bids a man see God among the mountains. It leads him to see the drama of our redemption, and to show the romance of our religion. In any community today this kind of interpreter will gain a hearing, and in time get a following.

Like the prophet, cultivate the spirit of optimism. Despite clouds on the horizon he looked forward to the coming of the Shepherd Prince. So must the preacher of today turn to Christ for the fulfillment of hopes and dreams that center in the gospel. "This man shall be our peace." However dark the signs of the times, God still rules.

87

"Christ shall have dominion over land and sea." Where but in Him can anyone find a basis for prophetic optimism like that of Micah?

As a young minister, begin now to make ready for a number of sermons from Micah next season. Spend the intervening weeks getting acquainted with this humble prophet from the country. You will enjoy preaching those sermons, and the people will thank you for introducing them to this believer in the average man. Better still, they should grow into the likeness of Him whom Micah foresaw as one of the common people.

CHAPTER V

Isaiah

THE HERALD OF GOD TO THE NATION

ISAIAH HAS LONG SINCE BECOME THE MOST FAMOUS OF all the prophets. In the New Testament the quotations from the book that bears his name outnumber those from any other prophetic source. In more recent times, among the vast majority of those who love the Bible, this man has become the favorite seer. Today whenever anyone speaks of a prophet, the name of Isaiah comes to mind first. He attained such distinction chiefly because of eloquence, but he had countless other gifts and graces. Indeed, Isaiah could have qualified as a genius, with vast and varied powers, all under the control of one who set his face like a flint as he strove to do the will of God.

With such glowing estimates many scholars would agree. The two statements that follow come from learned men of yesterday who differed widely. Isaiah was "distinguished less by any special excellence than by the symmetry and perfection of his powers." [1] "With Isaiah sank into the grave the greatest classic of Israel. Never did the speech

[1] See A. F. Kirkpatrick, *The Doctrine of the Prophets* (London: Macmillan and Co., 3rd ed., 1901) p. 144; cf. p. 147.

of Canaan pour forth with more brilliant splendor and triumphant beauty than from his lips. He has a strength and power of language, a majesty and sublimity of expression, an inexhaustible richness of feeling and stirring imagery, that overwhelms the reader, nay, fairly bewilders him." [2]

Isaiah served as a statesmen and a reformer, a historian and a theologian, a poet and an orator. In his own eyes and in those of his Lord this man stood out most of all as a preacher. The style of his written work has become the admiration if not the despair of speakers and writers. Especially does he excel in the use of imagination. He still lives as the spokesman of God to the nation. As such he will appear in this chapter.

The Facts About Isaiah's Career

Few of us today understand the book of Isaiah. We seldom read it as a whole, and then not with a sense of mastery. We may know passages here and there, and turn to them with ease. We might as well pride ourselves on knowing the geography of the United States because we have visited Mount Mitchell and Pike's Peak. Without some acquaintance with Isaiah's background we cannot expect to comprehend many of his warnings and promises.

[2] See Carl H. Cornill, trans., *The Prophets of Israel* (Chicago: Open Court Publishing Co., 1907), p. 68.

On the contrary, if we study his prophecies in the light of Hebrew history, we may hope for rich returns.

The facts about Isaiah appear almost exclusively in the first part of the work that bears his name. Even there, as a rule, he refers to himself only in passing. He appears to have come from noble stock, to have received a first-class education, and to have won distinction at the court in Jerusalem. As a prophet he served during the latter part of the eighth century before Christ; that is, during the golden age of prophecy, an age to which he brought the brightest luster. He appears to have begun prophesying about 740 B.C. and to have continued until about 700 B.C.

Throughout those forty years the land of Judah sorely needed a spokesman from God. During long years of peace under King Uzziah farmers had filled their barns to bursting. Barons had accumulated treasures in the way of land and money, which they used to oppress the poor. Vying with one another in all sorts of display, the so-called upper classes kept running to every excess of riot. Also did their womenfolk excel in wanton display of charms, and in enticements to sexual sin.

All the while the nation was becoming entangled with vaster powers which looked down on wee Judah and her religion. By ignoring her God, so as to become like the neighbors, Judah was undermining the moral foundations on which the fathers had built the state and the church. About midway in Isaiah's career the Northern Kingdom

91

had gone into captivity, never to return. Would Judah
also suffer such a fate? To all such portents of oncoming
doom the rulers seemed blind. When Isaiah pointed out
a way to escape from a fate like that of Israel, the rulers
in Jerusalem gave little heed. Over against this black background let us look at some of his messages, with special
reference to the needs of today. In these few we should
find the keynotes of his entire ministry.

THE REASONABLENESS OF OUR RELIGION

In the opening chapter the first twenty verses may lead
to a sermon about "The Reasonableness of Our Religion."
As a gateway into this field use part of verse 18, "Come
now, and let us reason together, saith the Lord." In the
midst of the mountains God summons His people to a conference. First of all He expostulates with them about the
unreasonableness of their sins. How can such rebellion
against God, with sickness of soul, fail to bring calamities?

Then the Lord turns to the unreasonableness of their
public worship. Then as now, God sanctioned forms of
worship. Through the regular use of such forms He
brought Isaiah into the prophetic office. Still the Lord
moved the seer to protest against sacrificial ceremonies as
substitutes for righteousness. Woe be to us churchfolk
when means of grace become ends of selfishness! If this
note sounds forth from prophet after prophet, so does
the evil continue from age unto age.

Last of all comes the climactic truth. The reasonableness of repentance! "Cease to do evil; learn to do well." Repentance means far more than an emotional upsurge, quickly to subside. When people repent, they change their whole attitude toward God and toward sin.[3] They determine henceforth to live according to the will of God and to serve in His name. Repentance means, not simply turning over a new leaf, but beginning a new life. So it appears that preaching from Isaiah calls for the pulpit use of doctrine, but never apart from duty. Strive not merely to entertain, or even to inspire, but also to instruct and to move Godward.

The latter part of this golden text may lead to a different kind of message. "Though your sins be as scarlet, they shall be as white as snow." These words full of prophetic beauty suggest a working rule for study and pulpit. Let the tone color of the passage determine the tone color of the sermon. When the sacred writer speaks of God's cleansing power in terms of snow on Mount Hermon, deal with the truth imaginatively. Lead the hearer to see the beauty of a spotless life, and to desire the cleansing God waits to bestow.

Such a text and subject call for a message full of quiet beauty. According to psychology, when a man's heart begins to move, his words tend to flow. If the Spirit of God moves on the heart of a prophet, his words suggest

[3] See William D. Chamberlain, *The Meaning of Repentance* (Philadelphia: Westminster Press, 1943).

something to see and feel, to do and become. On the contrary, if the man in the pulpit deals with such a truth unimaginatively, he may misrepresent the God of all beauty and grace. So it appears that pulpit exposition calls for more than exegesis of words and phrases. In order to interpret a truth from Isaiah, a man needs the soul of a poet. Fortunately, he may seek the guidance of the Spirit who led Isaiah to compose these words full of life, beauty, and saving power.

The use of imagination appears more fully in the fifth chapter, "The Parable of the Wild Grapes." Here Isaiah utters one of the two pure parables in the Old Testament.[4] The other one forms part of Nathan's rebuke to King David (II Sam. 12:1-6). Isaiah's parable relates to a vineyard; Nathan's to a lamb. In the Southern Kingdom the culture of grapes and the tending of sheep constituted the chief industries. In preaching about the duties of men the prophet of old drew his local color from the everyday concerns of his hearer. Once again Isaiah shows the preacher how to use imagination in lighting up a sermon.

With a few minor changes this parable would apply to our country today. In words full of beauty the prophet shows how the Lord has blessed His chosen people. In terms of a vineyard He has chosen the stock, prepared the soil, planted the vine, and nurtured it with care. Such a re-

---

[4] For a wider use of the term see Clarence E. Macartney, *The Parables of the Old Testament* (New York: Fleming H. Revell Co., 1916).

cital makes us think of our own early history. In view of all His bounty, the Lord of the American vineyard has a right to expect from our country "the fruit of the Spirit." What this means in American life today the interpreter can make clear after he has studied the latter part of chapter 5. However beautiful and moving his words, Isaiah always uses them to teach a doctrine or a duty. Often he does both.

Here he sets forth the doctrine of "election," and that for service. Like other Hebrew seers this one stresses the Lord's election of the people as a whole, rather than one by one. God has chosen and prepared the vineyard to bring forth the fruits of righteousness. In America, He wishes us to produce men and women of character, with homes like heaven; business on the basis of the Ten Commandments "interpreted by love"; and government according to the principles of His Kingdom. What other fruitage has the Lord a right to expect from the vineyard that He has blessed more than any other since the morning stars sang together at creation's dawn?

By way of contrast, what does the Lord behold today in His vineyard? Wild grapes! In the words of a novel full of filth, assembled from country slums—*Grapes of Wrath!* Without pausing to glance at these wild grapes, let us take for granted that they grow on every side of us here at home. In view of all our wild grapes the Lord holds out two alternatives. On the one hand He bids us repent and confess. This way would lead to a revival in our land. On the contrary, if we persist in bringing forth "grapes of wrath," He bids us look forward to judgment. What portents of doom the future has in store, God alone can know. This much He has made clear through Isaiah: the Lord wishes us to repent and turn from our evil courses. Then He would have us bring forth the sort of fruit for which He has set apart our nation and lavished on her the bounty of heaven. Which shall we choose, the will of God or "grapes of wrath"?

This parable suggests another working rule for the preacher today. A passage full of drama calls for a sermon full of action. A parable should lead to a message full of life and color, about persons of interest to the man in the pew. The action ought to involve struggle, or conflict, with increasing suspense. Out of it should come the solution of the problem in hand. For such a drama in a few words, read the parable of the wild grapes. Then let the same kind of drama appear in the sermon. Remember that an undramatic account of a moving passage would misrepresent this part of God's written Word. After hearing a discourse of the wrong kind a Britisher remarked that it consisted mainly of "longitude, latitude, and platitude."

THE YOUNG MAN AT WORSHIP

For dramatic action, swift and striking, the sixth chapter excels anything so far. Why it does not come at the beginning of the book, no one can say. The prophet tells about his call, which has become well known to us ministers. It ought also to interest our lay friends. Under God the hope for the Church of tomorrow depends largely on our securing the right sort of recruits for the ministry. Both in college and seminary many a young man ought to study this passage, and that on his knees. Whether or not he should become a minister of the gospel, he can learn much from this account of "A Young Man at Worship."

Young Isaiah comes to the sanctuary at a time of national uncertainty and dread, all of which he shares. He has grown to manhood under a king worthy of admiration. Now that Uzziah has died, the young man wonders what will befall the nation. He faces a crisis and he dare not meet it alone. So he comes to the Temple. In the House of the Lord he beholds a vision that seems not to touch the problem at hand. In forms that appeal to the imagination he learns to think of God as present and as holy. From this time onward for twoscore years Isaiah will preach nothing apart from the holiness of God. If in his old age anyone asks him to state in a single word the heart of all his prophetic ministry, Isaiah will answer "Holiness!"

Holiness means that God differs from all other persons, being high and lifted up in spiritual goodness and splendor. The revelation of God's holiness led to Isaiah's discovery of his own sinfulness, and that of his people. Most of all he became aware of sins with his lips. As a future prophet he would need to serve God with lips free from guile. So he beheld a vision of lips cleansed by fire, and that from the sacrificial altar. Then he heard a call to the service of the Lord. In response to that call the young man gave himself into the hands of God for life. Here we usually stop reading, but the prophet goes on to show the vision of God's judgment on the nation.

This passage sounds keynotes that ring out through all the ministry of Isaiah, often in the same order as here: the holiness of our God, the sinfulness of His people, the need of His cleansing, the call to His service, and the certainty of His judgment. These truths a young man ought to learn in the House of God. When he comes to the sanctuary with a heart full of uncertainty and fear, he may not receive answers to his inquiries about what lies round the next few bends in the roadway of life. Better than that, he can get right with God and then look to Him for guidance along every step of the way. With new peace in his heart he can sing with young John Henry Newman:

> I do not ask to see
> The distant scene—one step enough for me.

The first eight verses of the sixth chapter teach much about the sort of words to use in the pulpit. With a red pencil go through these verses and underline every word or phrase that suggests something to see, to feel, to do. Soon the page will begin to glow like a portion of the heavens at midnight. In the American Standard Version, among 215 words a student counted almost 50 with appeals to imagination. Would that every young preacher might learn to rely on nouns full of life and power, and verbs full of action and beauty. With "live words," fact words, action words, he would not need to depend on fuzzy and effeminate adjectives and adverbs. Make a list of these fifty words—such as flew, live coal, tongs, altar, touched, lips, and taken away. See if you can find in the entire passage a single descriptive adjective or adverb. Then go through the passage to see how any such superfluous word would mar the succession of motion pictures. What a passage for a case study in the use of words for the glory of the Lord!

THE COMING OF THE MESSIANIC KING

The same kind of beauty and power appears in Isaiah's messianic promises. Only one of them need concern us now, and that the noblest of them all (9:2-7). Here the prophet bids us rejoice in the coming King as "Wonderful Counsellor, Mighty God, Everlasting Father, Prince of Peace." These words full of power ring out at a climactic stage of Part I in Handel's *Messiah*.[5] They might serve as the text for the first of a short evening series during the Advent season, about "The Gospel in Handel's

[5] The chorus sings, "Wonderful, Counsellor," but the Hebrew parallelism seems to call for the other rendering, "Wonderful Counsellor."

Messiah." Thank God for a faith that leads us to sing at Christmas time and throughout the year!

In this passage the first part sings about "The Religion of Joy" (9:2), joy that begins with the coming of light. In Holy Scripture darkness serves as a symbol of ignorance, evil, and death. Light speaks of wisdom that issues from God, power that abides in Him, guidance that He gives, and splendor that He bestows. For many such reasons our hymns about the Advent season and the birth of Christ sing about Him in terms of light.

> Watchman, tell us of the night,
> What its signs of promise are.

This hymn has to do with the coming of Christ as the dayspring from on high. The same note of triumphant gladness rings out from the noblest of our Christmas songs, "Hark! the Herald Angels Sing":

> Hail the heav'n-born Prince of Peace!
> Hail the Sun of righteousness!
> Light and life to all He brings,
> Risen with healing in His wings.

Much the same note of joy sounds out from the harvest field (9:3). Among those Hebrews the harvest season meant the happiest time of all the year. The season brought them together from far and near, to rejoice in the bounty of God's "good earth," and to share joys with those they

100

loved. Members of the family circle would renew recollections of years bygone and make plans for days to come. What a foreshadowing of Christmas as the home-coming time! Would that all our Yuletide joys might center in Christ as the Incarnate Son of God! What a season for the ingathering of souls! Why not let the year's evangelistic appeal culminate at Christmas, at Easter, and at Pentecost?

The prophet also sings about triumph in battle (9:3c-5). This part of the messianic song perplexes some of us, and we pass it by. We might understand it better in Moffatt's rendering: "The stamping warrior's boot, the blood-stained war attire, shall all of them be burnt, as fuel for the fire." What welcome tidings for a people who often suffered from "war's wild alarms"! The coming King would usher in a reign of peace and good will. In terms of today,

> The cannon then shall cease to roar,
> And the only sound from its rusty throat
> Shall be a wren's or a bluebird's note,
> And nations shall learn war no more.

Alas, almost 2,700 years have flown by, and still we have not begun to see the fulfillment of Isaiah's vision about peace on earth.[6]

All these joys have to do with the birth of Christ. They

---

[6] For a still more remarkable vision (2:2-4) see the discussion of the parallel passage in Micah 4:2-5, pp. 74-75, *supra*.

101

lead up to the main part of the prophecy, which relates to His character. He alone can reign forever as King because He alone has the wisdom, the power, the timelessness, and the goodness of our God. These truths about the King shine out more clearly and more fully in the New Testament, where the doctrine appears as the Deity of Christ. In all His glory the Messianic King deserves to sit on the throne of the universe. When at last He begins to have His way throughout the world He died to redeem, we shall have peace on earth, and not until that time. So let us keep on praying, "Thy kingdom come."

This line of thought came out during a conversation on an Atlantic liner. A leading Scottish divine said to a still more distinguished American statesman, "What does your country need? What can be wrong with the United States?" The Scotsman was thinking of misgovernment in our cities and of immorality everywhere among us.

After the statesman had thought a little, he answered, "America needs an emperor."

"Sir, as a leader of American thought and life do you confess that your form of government has failed and that your country needs an absolute monarch?"

"Yes," replied the statesman, "America needs an emperor, and His name is Jesus Christ."

America has an Emperor, and so has the world. His name is Jesus Christ. Would that every knee might bow before Him and every heart acclaim Him King!

THE HERALD OF GOD TO THE NATION

Another messianic passage (11:1-9) also deserves to be well known. Here the prophet appeals to the imagination in a fashion equally striking and, from our point of view, more in keeping with the external facts about the coming Redeemer. The former passage declared that He would come in glory; the words now before us tell of His lowly origin. Here the prophet speaks in terms of what we know as the orchard, or perhaps the wood lot. All the while he looks forward to the coming of an invading host which will take the people captive and despoil their land. Amid all this coming devastation "a remnant" will survive. Out of this remnant will come the Messianic King.

After every invasion of Palestine many a farmer could look out and see raw stumps where before he had looked on growing trees. In our own time the Turks did their utmost to make the hills of the Holy Land barren. In recent days the Zionists have been striving to reforest hills denuded of trees. Over against such a background any lover of an oak tree can see what the prophet meant when he sang: "A shoot will spring from the roots of Jesse, and a sprout from his roots will bear fruit" (Smith-Goodspeed). Where many another tree gives up hope and dies after it loses everything but roots and stump, an oak sends

103

out shoots, any one of which may develop into a full-grown tree.[7]

Despite His lowly origin, or perhaps because of it, the coming King was to usher in the golden age. Because the Spirit of the Lord rested upon Him, He would embody all the wisdom and power needful in God's Ruler. In terms of our day, all too prosaic, He would have untold intellectual powers, a wealth of practical wisdom, and, best of all, religious insight (vss. 2-3). With this Godlike equipment in the way of character He would rule with righteousness and truth (vss. 4-5), so that the Lord God would have His way throughout the world. For a modern version of these glowing promises turn to Isaac Watts's hymn, "Joy to the world! the Lord is come."

Again in terms of the farm and the wood lot, the prophet sings about the coming Ruler's influence over wild beasts of the forest and even over serpents in their holes (vss. 6-9). The writer assumes that all nature has suffered from the ravages of sin, and that all created things will share in the transforming power of the Redeemer. Where Watts leads us to sing, "No more let . . . thorns infest the ground," Isaiah is much bolder. He would have us think of friendship and helpfulness between the lamb and the wolf, the cow and the bear, the babe and the viper. Best of all, as an artist shows us on canvas, in that

---

[7] Under still another figure the truth of His lowly origin appears in Isa. 53:2.

coming day a little child will lead tame cattle from their stalls and wild beasts from their dens in the forest.

What does all of this mean today? At least it reminds us that the powers of earth have become known as wild beasts. For example, think of the Lion and the Bear. Many of us admire the one nation and dread the other. Whatever our sympathies and our fears, strong nations have often reached out to capture and devour peoples that have seemed to us childlike. In as far as we can see, the end is not yet. All the while the messianic promises shine out from the Book. In fullness and glory they may relate to another era beyond our own, in the misty realm that we know as eschatology, but here and now they set up ideals that have to do with world missions. For a present-day commentary, turn again to the hymnal. There think of the song:

> Hail to the brightness of Zion's glad morning,
> Long by the prophets of Israel foretold.

How does the prophet expect the Lord to bring about such a transformation? He gives the answer in the closing words of this vision, where he makes clear that the promise has to do with all the world: "[The wild beasts of earth] will do no harm or destruction on all my holy mountain; for the land will have become full of the knowledge of the Lord, as the waters cover the sea" (11:9 Smith-Goodspeed). If in days bygone we followers of the Messianic

King had done our part in making Him known over all
the earth, we might now witness a partial fulfillment of
these promises. As we look out over the unknown mor-
row, we have to choose between the ideals of the prophet
and the practices of the jungle. Again and again our so-
called Christian nations have resorted to the ways of the
jungle. Now let them turn to the Lord. Before we dare to
pronounce His ways impractical, let us give them a fair
trial over land and sea.

The Power of God's Minority

This prophecy about the shoot springing up from the
stump of the oak has much to do with Isaiah's teachings
about "the remnant." Both before and after the song
about the coming golden age the prophet tells about the
remnant that will survive after the nation as a whole has
gone into captivity.[8] In our English tongue, unfortunately,
the term remnant tells of something mean and poor, if not
vile and pernicious. The term suggests "an insignificant
part or piece left from a former whole, as the remnant of
a once powerful army, or a sale of remnants of cloth." [9]
Sometimes the prophet uses the term in this sense, but in
the passages now before us the word means almost ex-
actly the reverse. It points to the sort of excellence that

[8] In the good sense of the word remnant the same Hebrew root appears
in Isa. 10:20, 21, 22; in 11:11, 16. Cf. 37:4, 32; also 46:3.
[9] See *Webster's Dictionary of Synonyms* (Springfield, Mass.: G. and C.
Merriam Co., 1942), a work that proves useful every day.

deserves to endure. The remnant here means God's minority; in the best sense of the phrase, "the survival of the fittest"! In the coming days of which the prophet sings the hope for the world, under God, will rest with His minority.

A people soon to face exile, if not extinction, needed such a message of hope.

> Lift up your hearts.
> We lift them up unto the Lord.

Like the Northern Kingdom, the one to the south would suffer for her sins. Unlike Israel, Judah would not become extinct. Like a Syrian river that for a while flows along in its bed, and then all at once disappears, never again to emerge, the Northern tribes had already ceased to have "a local habitation and a name." On the contrary the Southern Kingdom would live on as a church, though not as a state. In the providence of God His minority would live on until at length it brought forth the Messianic King.

Not only does the teaching about the remnant stand out in the prophecies of Isaiah. This aspect of prophecy has also begun to engage the attention of New Testament scholars. Over in Britain one of them, T. W. Manson, stresses the importance of the Remnant by spelling the word with a capital. On the Continent these promises about God's minority ought to mean still more. In our

homeland too the utterances about the remnant ought to
loom larger than ever before in our history. Have we not
witnessed the Church in some lands being forced to go
underground, and in every country the people of God
being treated as a minority? If anyone today would live
in hope, he must look up to God.

The significant history of Israel is the history of the
Remnant, that is, the history of the minority in Israel who
remain loyal to the covenant and to their covenant God. This
remnant, always there even when unobserved by men, is
manifested in times of religious crisis. The nature of the crisis
determines the way in which it will show itself. . . . In the
days of Isaiah and the Assyrian menace, it is the company of
people who accept the prophet's message, turn to God, and
wait for His deliverance.
    This idea of the remnant plays its part in the Gospel story.
Jesus gathers round Himself a company of people who should
embody the Remnant ideal as He sees it. . . . They are not
called to create the remnant, but to join it; not to build or
bring the Kingdom of God, but to receive it and enter it.[10]

In the writings of a practical churchman this idea of the
remnant also emerges. In discussing the recent history of
Germany, and the hope for her future, Bishop Henry K.
Sherrill points to this truth about the remnant. With him
other world leaders would agree, though by no means
in every detail:

[10] See T. W. Manson, *The Church's Ministry* (London: Hodder &
Stoughton; Philadelphia: Westminster Press, 1949), pp. 15-16.

108

Many of these German churchmen had proved their loyalty to Christ by spending months to years in concentration camps. . . . In this minority of clergy and people is to be found the hope of Germany and that those who have passed through this ordeal-by-fire unscathed in spirit if not in body have much to give us of other nations and Churches. But that does not change the hard fact that they were a very small minority.[11]

In every land where the followers of the Nazarene constitute a minority, what course shall the leaders of the Church pursue? That of prophetic optimism or that of pagan defeatism? Under God, the hope for the world of tomorrow still rests with the Church as a minority group,[12] and with ministers as the leaders of the Church. In preparing for such leadership no pastor can do better than saturate his soul in these prophecies of Isaiah. Not only can the local interpreter find here a wealth of truth for sermons. He can also enter into the spirit of the man who helped to prepare the remnant of God's people for the advent of their Messianic King. He could do that because he refused to despair about the blessing of God on the minority that we know as the Church.

The first twelve chapters of Isaiah end with a note of prophetic optimism. "With joy shall ye draw water out of

[11] See *The Church's Ministry in Our Time* (New York: Charles Scribner's Sons, 1949), pp. 10-11.
[12] See Harry E. Fosdick, "The Hope of the World in Its Minorities," *The Hope of the World* (New York: Harper & Bros., 1933) pp. 1-10.

the wells of salvation." (12:3.) What a text for both pastor and people! In their setting these words provide the basis for a message at Thanksgiving time. All the year round they will serve as an illuminated motto on the wall of the pastor's study, over against that copy of Sargent's "Prophets." Whenever the young minister looks at the motto, he may imagine that he hears a thoughtful lay friend protesting, "Sir, thou hast nothing to draw with, and the well is deep" (John 4:11*a*).

The Judgment on Godless Rulers

In the same book with messianic promises and glowing words about the remnant Isaiah also paints gloomy scenes of judgment. Thus he shows the contrast between the ideal and the actual. On page after page, especially in chapters 13 through 27, he deals largely with the Lord's judgment on other nations, which need not concern us now. In chapter 28 he turns more directly to his own people. Here he condemns the sins and excesses of the nation's rulers and others who sit in high places. Except for details here and there the same strictures apply in our own country today. What a passage for preaching during the period before a national election! By a strange coincidence Election Day comes at a season of the year when the pastor most fitly interprets one of the prophetic oracles.

The first part of the chapter shows "The Folly of Drunken Politicians" (28:1-13). The prophet refers to

110

rulers in Israel whose debauchery has helped to hasten the captivity of the Northern Kingdom. Then he turns on the rulers of Judah, with the prophets and priests. Those so-called leaders keep defiling themselves with strong drink. They let liquor befuddle their senses. They reel and stagger about like men at their wits' end. These drunken "leaders" even befoul the tables of the Lord with their vomit, and then wallow in their filth. Not content with acting like swine in the sty, they begin to make sport of the prophet who dares to rebuke their sins. In the Hebrew the report of their drunken song has an insulting lilt that the Smith-Goodspeed translation tries to reproduce in English:

> To whom would he impart knowledge,
> To whom explain the message?
> Babes just weaned from milk,
> Just drawn from the breasts?
> For it is rule by rule, rule by rule,
> Line by line, line by line,
> A little here and a little there.

The fury of the prophet's attack increases. In the central part of the chapter (28:14-22) he shows "The Folly of a Covenant with Hell." Because the rulers have made a bargain with destruction and death, God will send the destroyer, who will deprive the land of its freedom. In large measure the same indictment holds true in our country today. Our lawmakers have made a covenant with hell

111

in the shape of the liquor traffic. In many localities those in power have made similar bargains with gambling and immorality. Should the minister and the local church keep silent while the government permits lovers of money to debauch our sons and daughters with strong drink, along with enticements to gambling and sexual sin? Somebody must have made a covenant with death and hell.

In the heart of this chapter about judgment on sin shines out a verse that provides a basis of hope. Hope in God! Despite drunken rulers and godless bargains the Lord still reigns. "Behold, I lay in Zion for a foundation a stone, a tried stone, a precious corner-stone of sure foundation: he that believeth shall not be in haste." (28:16.) Both in Church and in state

> Christ is made the sure foundation,
> Christ the head and cornerstone.

How He wishes us to deal with wickedness in high places, He alone can tell. In all such things He would have us rely on Him with "the repose of a settled faith." "He that believeth shall not make haste."

THE POWER OF A GODLY LEADER (32:1-8)

In contrast with such a gloomy chapter the artist paints a word picture of an oasis in the desert. "A man shall be as a hiding-place from the wind, and a covert from the tempest, as streams of water in a dry place, as the shade

112

of a great rock in a weary land." (32:2.) This one man stops the drift away from God, and in place of shifting sands begins to create an oasis in the desert. For an example of such an influential citizen take Boaz in the little town of Bethlehem. At a time when the morals of the land had sunk to the lowest level this "country gentleman" helped to make his community the best place of its size and sort. "The noble man planneth noble things, and on noble things doth he stand." (32:8 Smith-Goodspeed.)

For another example turn to *Sam Higginbottom, Farmer*.[13] Once as a missionary in India he wrote to thank an Ohio congregation for a generous gift. The chief lay officer replied:

We should thank you. You have opened our eyes to a world in need. Our Christianity has become more vital since we have seen the far horizon. Before you came I usually put a quarter or a fifty-cent piece into the annual missionary plate. When you talked about plows and harrows and threshing machines, I saw that my quarter would not go very far. I have tried, therefore, to give each year the price of a plow or a cow.[14]

Not only in the realm of missions does the world require strong men as leaders. For example, take our candidates for the Presidency. During a recent campaign a wise observer, Justice Brandeis of the Supreme Court, ap-

[13] Under this title, an autobiography (New York: Charles Scribner's Sons, 1949).
[14] *Ibid.*, p. 109.

113

praised the men running against the one in office. The jurist insisted that no one of the competing candidates compared with the men arrayed against Andrew Jackson a hundred years ago: John Quincy Adams, Henry Clay, John C. Calhoun, and Daniel Webster. With many times more inhabitants, and with far more perplexing problems, our country today has not leaders strong enough, wise enough, and good enough to stop the drift and make an oasis in the desert. In large measure our so-called civilization has failed. At last we should try God's way of producing strong men by His blessing on home and church.

THE SERMONS FROM ISAIAH

So we might go on, but we have proceeded far enough to make clear both the difficulty and the fascination of preaching much from Isaiah. A young pastor may well think twice before he embarks on such an adventure. Some passages he can scarcely hope to understand. Others he may not feel able to use in meeting the needs of the hearers today. In the book as a whole he can find riches so vast and so varied that he may feel confused, if not overwhelmed. Even so, let him persevere in study of these oracles. As long as he lives he will thank God if early in the ministry he becomes well acquainted with the writings of this major prophet. In any such undertaking a few practical counsels may help the young interpreter in getting his bearings. They come from the experience of one who blundered about before he found a way to deal with the book of Isaiah in the study and in the pulpit.

Allow abundance of time for mastering the book. Before a man preaches much from any part of the Bible, he ought to understand that portion as a whole. Otherwise he might fail to convey the message with its unique tone color. For the mastery of Isaiah a young man does well to allow a year or more. Even if he does not preach for a while from the book he will find that these morning studies day after day tone up his entire system and help him in dealing with simpler parts of Holy Scripture. If merely for his own sake, a young minister needs to use all his intellectual muscles in mastering such a difficult part of the Bible.

In the book of Isaiah dare to select and omit. Altogether apart from questions about authorship, anyone can see that chapters 1 to 39 differ from those that follow. Why not concentrate on this first main part of the book? Here you will find more than enough to keep you busy for months. In the first thirty-nine chapters single out those that deal mainly with Judah. As for the passages chiefly about her neighbors (chs. 13–27) why not leave them for later study of the book? As a result of such fencing off you will set yourself the task of dealing with only twenty-four chapters, and these not the most difficult in Isaiah.

After you know these chapters well, dare to preach from the book a few sermons leading up to Christmas. In

115

the bulletin request the people to read designated chapters from Isaiah before they come to church each Lord's Day after Thanksgiving.[15] Remember that many of them admire this book and wish to know it better. Without changing the pulpit into a platform for professorial lectures, you can help the layman to see why the book of Isaiah looms large in the New Testament. After a few messages from this royal prophet you can turn with zest to kindred passages in Matthew about the birth of the Redeemer.

In selecting the texts for a few sermons from Isaiah give the preference to words full of power to uplift. Remember that this prophet excels in use of imagination and that the lay hearer ought to approach these writings as the outpouring of a prophetic soul. Without calling attention to how you preach, be sure that the tone color of each message accords with that of the words from Isaiah. In the first few sermons you may not get beyond the eleventh chapter, with its "Gospel That Transforms." Very well! If you enter into the spirit of each passage, and then preach about it with prophetic enthusiasm, the people will keep asking when you plan to give them still more sermons from the seer whom many persons love best of all those that stand out in Sargent's frieze of the prophets.

[15] For an example of this method see *The Memoirs of John R. Sampey* (Nashville: The Broadman Press, 1947), p. 167.

CHAPTER VI

Isaiah—Continued

THE GOSPEL IN THE OLD TESTAMENT

NOW WE COME TO MOUNTAIN PEAKS OF PROPHECY. no-where in the Old Testament do many of us find so much of the gospel truth that shines out more strongly from the New. In passing from the earlier parts of Isaiah anyone can sense a change of climate, beginning with chapter 40. In those earlier chapters we found messages of warning and judgment, with an occasional word of hope. Here we have messages full of assurance and hope, with an occasional glimpse of darker truths. There the prophet addressed people headed for exile and heedless of the yawning abyss. Here he writes to a people upon whom judgment has fallen, making many of them humble and submissive. Who can wonder that hosts of us love some of these later chapters more than any others in the Old Testament,[1] excepting certain psalms?

These facts about differences of purpose and tone color raise a question about authorship. That problem need engage us at present only to make clear that the

---

[1] For a much less favorable appraisal of these later chapters see Pfeiffer, *op. cit.*, pp. 449-81.

117

writer of these later chapters seems to have addressed people in exile, people who sorely needed the gospel of God's comfort. These facts also suggest much about the strategy of the pulpit today. In times when everyone seems to prosper, at least in possession of things, stress the need of humility and repentance. In times of adversity, after the hour of judgment has come, and many have become penitent, sound a message full of hope and cheer. In either case the work of the pulpit consists mainly in the preaching of Bible doctrine. In preparing messages of comfort base everything on the character of God.

THE GOSPEL OF GOD'S COMFORT (CH. 40)

The fortieth chapter sounds the "gospel of comfort," which issues from Bible teaching about God. To comfort means to strengthen hearts in Him. This entire chapter breathes a message of comfort, assurance, and hope, because it all centers round the theme "Behold Your God!" (40:9.) In any such message about deliverance from exile, sorrow, or anything else, the interpreter ought to make clear his answer to the questions: How do you know? Why do you feel sure? This chapter as a whole and in every part gives the answer: The assurance of our gospel depends on the character of our God.[2]

The first eleven verses bring the peace of God to the

[2] See Norman H. Snaith, "The Prophets of the Exile," *Religion in Life,* Winter, 1949-50, pp. 83-91.

heart, in the present-day sense of the word. According to the original Hebrew the second verse begins: "Speak to the heart of Jerusalem," a form of sound words that any young pastor might adopt as a motto today. In the first eleven verses—which deserve more attention than we can give them now—comfort flows from truths about the compassion of God. The opening verse calls for a message about "The Bible Basis of Comfort." It all rests on the assurance of sins forgiven, and of God's will accepted. This opening section consists of four brief paragraphs containing the messages of four herald voices, each of which would provide materials for a moving sermon. "The Voice of God's Comforter." (40:1.) "The Voice of the Evangelist." (40:3.) "The Voice of the Undying Word." (40:8.) "The Voice of the Kind Shepherd." (40:11.) In the next section the prophet will sing about the majesty of the Most High. Here the stress falls on His tenderness. "The Gentleness of Our God." (40:11.) The tenderness of the shepherd with wee lambs and with expectant mothers would mean all the more to people in exile, as they kept thinking about flocks grazing on the hills in the homeland far away.

The main portion of the chapter (40:12-26) appeals to the head rather than the heart. More than almost any other portion of the Old Testament these verses have to do with doctrine, and that about God. The facts about the Most High, as we of today sometimes forget, provide undergirding for the entire Scriptures, both in the Old Testament and in the New. The stress here falls on the wisdom, the power, and the majesty of our God, but not in such prosaic terms. After a series of questions that few of us can answer, the prophet sings about "The God of All the Nations" (40:15.) What an opening for a sermon about world missions! Like evangelism here at home, missions overseas grow out of the Bible teachings about our God.

The young pastor will find it easier to deal with the closing verses. In terms of popular psychology—which makes these facts seem all too simple—the stress now falls on God's appeal to the will. Verse 28 calls for a message about "The Perseverance of Our God," a truth that undergirds both Testaments. For example, the Apostle writes: "He who began a good work in you will perfect it until the day of Jesus Christ" (Phil. 1:6). Isa. 40:28 voices much the same truth, and with still more poetic fervor. At other times the pulpit stresses the beginnings of redemption, or else the consummation at the final return of our Lord. Here the text calls for emphasis on what lies between Alpha and Omega. The wonder of God's persevering grace sounds forth from the hymn, "O Love That Wilt Not Let Me Go." This points to one believer, but the words of the seer relate to the Church. The perseverance of our God affords the Church her only assurance that the Kingdom will ever triumph. In the resulting message be careful to base everything on this Bible doctrine, as it concerns the character of God. Preach about "The Almighty Grip That Never Lets Go."

The climax of this golden chapter comes in well-known words about "Varieties of Religious Experience." "They that wait for the Lord shall renew their strength; they shall mount up with wings as eagles; they shall run, and not be weary; they shall walk, and not faint." (40:31.) In pointing out three stages in the experience of the saints the sacred writer may seem to have erred. As sophomores in college some of us would have tried to "improve" the words, to make them climactic. Thinking perhaps of the way an automobile or an airplane picks up speed after a slow start, we would have the saints begin by walking, then resort to running, and at last venture into flying.

The prophet never would sacrifice truth for a verbal climax. As a man of God he secured both, for he pictured three stages in the order of increasing difficulty. Some interpreters see here three stages in a good man's life: from youth with its ecstatic visions, through middle age with its achievements, and into old age with its quiet plodding. This interpretation may never have occurred to the writer himself, but still the analogy holds true. More probably the sacred writer looked at certain stages in the experience of God's people, whatever their years. Whichever interpretation you adopt, preach only one, and do not allude to the other. Only one series of word pictures in any sermon! Soar! Run! Walk!

To those who rely upon Him the Lord gives grace for the hour of ecstatic vision. Assuredly this experience may come in youth, but why not include all the young in heart? More often He blesses faith's pilgrim in times of progress and joy. Best of all, the Lord bestows grace when the soul cannot soar, or even run, but must plod along through mud and slime, or else through sand and heat. The hour of vision comes only occasionally; it may be only once in a lifetime. The days of swift progress do not last long; but the weeks and months of dull, drab drudgery, with pale, gray days of endurance, may lengthen into years. Then, if ever, you need God.

A man may pass through all these experiences in a single year, or even less. At a summer conference in the mountains he may feel lifted up so as to capture the secrets of the stars. During weeks that follow he may taste the joys of going forward gladly in doing the will of God. Before summer comes again he may have to endure drudgery with no mingling of delight. For such a child of God, as for an automobile, the chief test of power comes in low gear. For a living example of such experiences think of the apostle Paul. Once he was caught up into paradise, where he heard things he could never tell. Afterward, no doubt, he met with joy in doing the will of God. Then he had to struggle along while he endured a thorn in the flesh. So he learned much the same lesson as in Isa. 40:31:

"My grace is sufficient for thee: for my power is made perfect in weakness" (II Cor. 12:9).

GOD'S CURE FOR DISORDERS OF THE SOUL

After chapter 40 many passages would lead to sermons. Some of them would go together as a series about God's ways of healing soul disorders. The best of these passages have to do with the Servant of the Lord, the noblest of which concern the coming Messiah. For example, "A bruised reed shall he not break, and the smoking flax shall he not quench." (42:3a King James Version.) "Christ's Way with a Damaged Soul." What could seem weaker than a reed bruised and bent down, or more worthless than a lamp that smokes and will not shine? Who could use a bruised reed in fashioning an organ pipe or a clarinet, a fishing pole or a walking stick? Cast it on the ash heap! As for a lamp that smokes, put it out! So the world deals with what it terms the "weak and the worthless." The world believes in "survival of the fittest."

How different the ways of our Lord! Behold the Son of God in the midst of the world's scrap heap, gathering up damaged souls,[3] and making them ready for service in the Kingdom. Watch Him fanning into a flame the zeal that has almost disappeared from one who has quit trying to do good. The words of this text come with all the more

---

[3] See Gamaliel Bradford, *Damaged Souls* (Boston: Houghton Mifflin Co., 1923), p. 3. Also Harold Begbie, *Twice-Born Men.*

force in the light of what follows. There the Hebrew says that the Servant Himself shall never burn dimly or be bruised. He shall not become discouraged or quit. Once again behold the divine perseverance! In this message be sure to deal with one soul, as in the text.

Another passage tells about "God's Remedy for Fear" (43:1-3a). In days of exile these words came to God's children as a group. Today the text would also help any soul in distress. By altering the form of the first part, without affecting the sense, the preacher may stress four sayings for the fearful heart. (1) "I have formed thee." (2) "I have called thee." (3) "I will be with thee." (4) "I am the Lord thy God." For light upon these sayings turn to the hymn that Henry van Dyke declared many a congregation sang better than any other in the book:

> When thro' the deep waters I call thee to go,
> The rivers of woe shall not thee overflow. . . .
> When through fiery trials thy pathway shall lie,
> My grace, all-sufficient, shall be thy supply.

Once again, "I will gird thee, though thou hast not known me" (45:5). These unfamiliar words once led to a sermon that has become famous, "Every Man's Life a Plan of God" by Horace Bushnell. Note here, as in the text, the emphasis on the will of God for one man, who in the sermon proves to be the friend in the pew. However dark and hard the way, anyone can rest secure in the undergirding of God's Providence. This doctrinal discourse grows out of a proposition, or key sentence. A minister today would state the idea more simply, but he could not put into words a more uplifting truth:

God has a definite life-plan for every human person, girding him, visibly or invisibly, for some exact thing, which it will be the true significance and glory of his life to have accomplished.

What a truth to stabilize the soul! Here follow some of Bushnell's words near the end:

Young man, or woman, this is the day of hope to you. All your best opportunities are still before you. Now, too, you are laying your plans for the future. Why not lay them in God? Who has planned for you as wisely and faithfully as he? Let your life begin with him. Believe that you are girded by your God for a holy and great calling. . . . Take your burdens, and troubles, and losses, and wrongs, if come they must and will, as your opportunities, knowing that God has girded you for greater things than these. O, to live out such a life as God appoints, how great a thing it is!—to do the duties, make the sacrifices, bear the adversities, finish the plan, and then to say, with Christ (who of us will be able?)— "It is finished!" [4]

Another text had much to do with Charles H. Spurgeon: "Look unto me, and be ye saved, all the ends of the earth;

[4] See my anthology of master sermons, *The Protestant Pulpit* (New York and Nashville: Abingdon-Cokesbury Press, 1947), pp. 83-84, 85.

for I am God, and there is none else" (45:22). To us this may not seem evangelistic, but to young Spurgeon it brought the saving knowledge of Christ. At the age of twenty-two he issued the first of sixty-three volumes of his regular sermons. To head the list in this first volume he chose a message about Isa. 45:22. Anyone who wishes to tie up golden passages with well-known personages can preach here about "The Text of Charles H. Spurgeon."

Still another text once brought cheer to the household of a seminary professor. When he first gave up the pastorate, his wife did not protest, but she missed the joys of other days, and so did he. Three years later she heard one of the seniors preach about "The Church in the Hands of God." "I have graven thee upon the palms of my hands." (49:16.) With tears in her eyes she told her husband: "If you can have a part in training young men to preach like that, I shall thank God for your work as a teacher." Really he could not take the credit for that message, especially since he then taught Bible rather than homiletics. Only God can make a preacher, and He has done so in this case. Sometimes He employs professors as His agents.[5]

Let us look at the verse. To the Hebrews as a childlike people the hands symbolized power. What a person had

[5] For the sermon in another form, see William M. Elliott, "God's Engraved Hands," *Coming to Terms with Life* (Richmond, Va.: John Knox Press, 1944), pp. 66-74.

engraved upon his hands showed what he held most dear. In like manner today one might wear a wedding ring. In bald American prose the text means that God loves the Church, and keeps it ever before His eyes. Hence we often sing about Zion:

> Her walls before Thee stand,
> Dear as the apple of Thine eye,
> And graven on Thy hands.

Here we have truth that sings, doctrine set to music. Let the same hold true of the sermon. No lack of imagination and of power to uplift!

"The Secret of Effective Preaching" appears in Isa. 50:4a: "The Lord God hath given me the tongue of the learned, that I should know how to speak." This rendering of the old King James Version comes close enough to the original. As for stopping before the end of the verse, how else did our Lord in the synagogue at Nazareth preach from Isa. 60:1-2a?[6] Ideally, these words in Isa. 50:4 find fulfillment in the Master Preacher. Practically, they also afford working standards for every minister. Even after he has gone through the most approved schools of learning, he ought to receive every message from the Lord God. Prior to the speaking lips comes the hearing ear: "He wakeneth morning by morning, he wakeneth mine ear to hear

[6] Compare this message with Luke 4:18-19 as an object lesson of "Preaching from the Bible."

as the learned" (50:4*b* King James Version). What a text for the ordination sermon of a young minister! Such a message usually lacks the quality of surprise, and of sparkle.

"The Lord God will help me; therefore shall I not be confounded: therefore have I set my face like a flint, and I know that I shall not be ashamed." (50:7 King James Version.) To many of us these words point most of all to the coming Redeemer as He draws near to Golgotha. We do not mean that the writer thought directly about Him, but that He fulfilled these words in Holy Writ. "The Christ of the Flint Face." Sometime not long before Easter introduce the people to the masculine Christ as He set His face steadfastly toward Jerusalem, knowing that there He must die. Point out His courage in accepting the Cross, His perseverance in drawing daily nearer to Calvary, and His grace in transforming that symbol of shame and defeat into an emblem of triumph over sin and the grave. A masculine sermon about "The Christ of the Flint Face"!

The Gospel from the Cross

The gospel in the Old Testament sounds forth most clearly and wondrously from chapter 53. In many a pulpit Bible this page wears out sooner than any other, but no succession of interpreters can ever begin to exhaust the riches in this treasure house. In the Hebrew the poem con-

128

sists of five strophes, or stanzas, each a little longer than the one preceding because still more important. Since each strophe contains more than enough materials for a moving sermon, why not prepare a series of five? Then use them on the five evenings after Palm Sunday. In announcing this series looking up to Easter, ask the people to read this golden chapter again and again. Insist that they begin where the chapter ought to start: "Behold, my servant shall deal prudently" (52:13 King James Version). Better still, lead them to learn this poem by heart, and often say it aloud, catching the onward movement of the majestic rhythm.

In a message of this sort choose a text brief and striking. Then take the warp of the sermon from the surrounding paragraph, or strophe. Be sure to prepare a message full of doctrine set to music. Do not rest content merely with explaining a passage. Look on these words in light that streams from the New Testament, and do not preach as a Jewish rabbi. What an opportunity for a series about "The Drama of Our Redemption," or else more simply, "The Gospel in Five Words." With this latter title single out a word from each paragraph, and keep the five in climactic order. The terms that here follow may seem abstract, but the messages ought to glow with light from the face of our dying Redeemer. In the printed announcement omit the texts that appear below. Arrange the parts as carefully as in any other printed card of display:

The Gospel in Five Words

All the light of sacred story
Gathers round [His] head sublime.

Monday—The Gospel of Service (52:13*a*)
Tuesday—The Gospel of Suffering (53:3*ab*)
Wednesday—The Gospel of Substitution (53:5)
Thursday—The Gospel of Sacrifice (53:7*bc*)
Friday—The Gospel of Satisfaction (53:11*a*)

As a whole this chapter will test any man's ability to preach doctrine. Can he take the thought-forms of the prophet and translate them into the speech of our day, without dimming aught of their pristine luster? In this poem can he make the fivefold structure stand out as boldly as the five spans in a suspension bridge? In pointing to the "satisfaction" of the Saviour, can the interpreter forget other meanings of this word "satisfaction"—meanings that he may accept—in order to stress one fact? In glory today the Lord Christ rejoices because of what He did on Calvary. There He suffered according to the will of God. He suffered for others. He suffered as a prelude to eternal triumph. Do you wonder that He feels far more than satisfied with His sufferings? [7]

Before he dares to announce a series, even of five sermons, the novice may content himself with preaching from isolated verses, each with reference to its own back-

[7] For another treatment of this chapter see my *Preaching from the Bible*, pp. 146-50.

ground. Why not start with this: "He shall grow up before him as a tender plant, and as a root out of a dry ground" (53:2a)? Beautiful words, but what do they mean? A root does not grow out of ground devoid of water. Whenever a tender plant springs up in arid soil, the roots have come in touch with water. See here an opportunity to use what Charles H. Spurgeon called "the surprise power." When you start with such a text, be sure to deal with it in an old light. Relate the unknown to the known.

"The Mystery of Jesus Christ." Everyone loves a mystery, if only you can state it strongly, and also make it real. Among all of life's mysteries none can compare with that about Christ. On the human level who can begin to account for the Christ of the Cross? How does a biographer, such as Roland H. Bainton,[8] try to account for a mighty leader of men? On the basis of heredity and environment, education and culture, friendship and perhaps something else. Not all of these together can begin to account for Jesus Christ. "A root out of dry ground." "Can any good thing come out of Nazareth?" No, nothing but the Lord Jesus! In order to account for Him we must cease to move on the human level, and begin to think of God. Beneath the arid surface of life in Nazareth the roots of

[8] See his biography of Luther, *Here I Stand* (New York and Nashville: Abingdon-Cokesbury, 1950). A mastery of this book will do much to help any man in preaching from the prophets.

131

His being went down deep and kept in touch with living waters from the mountains of God. Still a mystery? Yea, verily, but a mystery full of wonder. The One who came from God!

"The Gospel in Personal Pronouns." (53:5.) In the original Hebrew the stress here falls repeatedly on the little word "our." As a rule the reader of Holy Scripture ought to emphasize nouns and verbs, especially verbs; but in this case the interpreter stresses the pronoun that points to us as sinners. The same holds true in some of our noblest hymns, though the pronouns there often appear in the singular. For example, "Rock of Ages, Cleft for Me." Well did Martin Luther declare that a man's ideas about religion appear in his use of pronouns. In this kind of sermon be careful not to change intimate pronouns into abstract statements about "man." Make the Cross of the Redeemer seem personal!

"With his stripes we are healed" (53:5c). "The Healing Power of the Cross." Repeatedly the Scriptures refer to sin as a deadly disease of the soul, and to salvation as a cure at the hands of the Divine Physician.[9] These words come to us as figures, but back of the figures loom facts that every lay hearer ought to know. Salvation means God's way of setting a man free from disorders of the soul, and making him ready for a life of joyous service. Not only

[9] See W. Mackintosh Mackay, *The Disease and Remedy of Sin* (New York: George H. Doran Co., 1919).

does the Lord save from sin and death. He also sets one free for life and service, both here and hereafter.

> Be of sin the double cure,
> Cleanse me from its guilt and power.

When the Christ of the Cross does all this, He does far more. He opens the way for a life of usefulness here and of hope for heaven.

"The Cross remaineth, and in the straits of the soul it makes its ancient appeal." So declared Matthew Arnold on his deathbed. In other days he had voiced ideas full of doubt, but when at last he looked death in the face he thought in terms of what he counted the noblest of all hymns: "When I Survey the Wondrous Cross." That hymn affords a running commentary on this "Gospel in Personal Pronouns."

THE VOICE OF THE EVANGELIST

Almost on a par with the Song of the Suffering Redeemer stands chapter 55. On the basis of the truths in that earlier passage an interpreter can use this later chapter in calling for repentance and returning to God. With dramatic skill the Hebrew evangelist rises in the market place where displaced persons gather to bewail their desolation. There he pleads with the disillusioned, the disheartened, the despairing. Today a pastor can behold such persons thronging city streets or walking in rural

133

lanes. He ought to know what they need—"things that money cannot buy." In a community with many newcomers, who feel uprooted and Godforsaken, preach about "The Gospel for Displaced Persons." (55:1.)[10]

Preach also about "The Bible Meaning of Repentance" (55:6-7). This text brings out two contrasting truths: what the Lord wishes the hearers to do, and what He promises to do in return. Note here both the urgency and the kindness of the imperative verbs. Seek! Call! Forsake! Turn! Seek the Lord and call upon Him. Forsake your evil ways and come to God. That sounds as though everything depended on us, but listen! "He will have mercy, and abundantly pardon." Once again, our entire gospel depends on the character of our God. In the sermon these two contrasting ideas ought to ring out again and again. When shall we interpreters learn from the prophets and their coming Redeemer the wisdom of meaningful repetition?

In the chapter as a whole this call for repentance forms a sort of dividing ridge. The verses preceding 6 and 7 tell about the hardships, the heartaches, and the hopelessness of those who try to muddle through life without God. The verses following the central ones tell about the freedom, the joy, and the hopefulness of those who have found their life in God. One of these closing portions calls for a message about "The Gospel in the Snow" (55:10-11)

[10] In this connection see pp. 58, 134, 151, 173.

or perhaps "The Gospel in the Rain." In those Eastern lands with their scarcity of water, people thought of snow on the mountains and of rain in the valleys as tokens of God's favor. This figure the prophet employs to show the blessing of God on the preaching and teaching of His Word.

This promise ought to gladden the heart of the pastoral evangelist at home and of the missionary abroad. In presenting the gospel, as in tilling a farm, God has arranged for effects to follow causes. He blesses the labor of the sower, the life in the seed, the strength of the soil, and the falling of the rain. In things of the Spirit, also, He waits to bless "the diligent use of the outward and ordinary means of grace." Both at home and abroad He wishes the messenger of the Evangel to toil as though everything depended on him and his efforts, while he prays because everything depends on God and His grace. The Lord alone can send the rain and the snow that make the soil ready for the coming harvest.

So we might go on through the remaining chapters. Instead of doing so, let us merely glance at verses here and there. In the first of these examples (60:1) note how the truths arrange themselves in the form of "thesis—antithesis —synthesis." In the resulting message do not employ such "pulpit jargon," but translate homiletical abstractions into words clear and luminous to the man in the street. Think of the last example (66:13) in terms of Mother's Day. In the

135

Hebrew the words run: "Like as a man whom his mother comforts, so will I comfort you." The prophet bids a man look up through his mother's love and see the wonders of God's comfort. These messages would serve better separately than as parts of a series.

The Glory of God as Light (60:1)
The Spirit of Christ's Preaching (61:1-2a)
The Prayers for a Man's Church (62:1)
The Power of God's Compassion (63:3)
The Power of God Among the Nations (64:1-2)
The Prophetic Vision of World Peace (65:25)
The Godlikeness of a Man's Mother (66:13)

We have gone far enough to see that no other portion of the Old Testament contains so much gospel truth and light as the latter part of Isaiah. If anyone wishes to become an effective preacher of the Evangel, let him live much in this mountain country. Here he will find abundance of materials for sermons full of doctrine, assurance, and hope. With these doctrines he can comfort the saints by strengthening their hearts in God. He can also use these portions of Holy Writ in presenting the claims of God to those that have lost their way out in the world full of woe. So by the blessing of the God about whom he preaches, both pastor and people will find here the truth that stabilizes souls and makes them strong to serve in the light of a hope that never grows dim.

CHAPTER VII

Jeremiah

THE EXPERIENCES OF A LONESOME SAINT

WE PROTESTANTS OUGHT TO KNOW AND LOVE JEREMIAH. In a sense we may think of all the true prophets as the Protestants of their day. Did they not stand out against the "Mother Church," and call on professors of religion for a thoroughgoing reformation of worship, doctrine, and morals? Did not all the prophets long and work for what we call a revival of religion? In all of that, Jeremiah stood second to none of the Hebrew seers. As a prophetic leader he appears to have accomplished more by saintliness than by all other means. If we believed in adoration of saints, this man could head the list. With the possible exception of Hosea, the so-called "weeping prophet" stands out above all the other saints of the Old Testament.

Why, then, has Jeremiah not become better known and loved? In his own time he did not win the favor of leaders in Church and state. He encountered opposition from kings and nobles, from priests and prophets, even from those he loved best—the common people. Up to the present hour he has not become popular. In contrast with Isaiah this other man has not won acclaim as a speaker or

137

writer. In Holy Scripture his prophetic writings cover more pages than any other book except the Psalms; but in works about the Bible, Jeremiah usually occupies a secondary place. Why so? Partly because his writings prove difficult to understand, and more because he has become known as a man of tears.

Many of us want our heroes to look happy. We have troubles enough of our own without wanting to share those of days bygone. Unconsciously we may have accepted Michelangelo's portrayal of Jeremiah as an "awestruck figure, in an attitude of hopeless despair." More probably we have adopted Sargent's conception of the Hebrew saint as a weakling full of gloom. Except for those who work their way through the Bible from cover to cover, few of us have read this man's book as a whole. Fewer still know it well enough to appraise its worth and revere the prophet whose writings Baruch or somebody else seems to have edited, in an order by no means chronological.

In almost every age a few readers have looked on Jeremiah as second to none of the Hebrew seers.

In his moments of greatest elevation Jeremiah is truly the prophet not of his own age but of one which has not yet dawned. He is the St. Paul of the Old Covenant. Jeremiah's prophetic glance penetrates the veil of coming centuries and reaches to the time when covenants and laws, priesthood and sacrifice, shall be forgotten; but the law of God

138

will be inscribed on the hearts of all.[1] Many a recent scholar shares this estimate. If it is correct, we should feel ashamed of neglecting the man whose writings occupy one fifteenth of the Old Testament.[2]

Most of us do not care for Jeremiah's style. We compare him with Isaiah and wonder why the later seer did not have so vivid an imagination. We think of passage after passage from the book of Isaiah, but how many can we name from this other writer? If we looked more closely, we should find more than a few passages worthy of note. Call his writings dull, if you must. Speak about the leaden wings of his fancy. But keep on plodding through this book, and you will find more than a few spots full of quiet beauty. Where save in the teachings of our Lord can you enjoy such homely figures as the girdle, the yoke, the two baskets of figs, and the broken bottle?

The Background of His Times

If we knew more about Jeremiah, we could appraise his work more fairly. Nowhere else in the Old Testament can we employ the historical method more profitably. Largely from his own writings we can learn more about him than about any other Hebrew seer. Unlike Isaiah, but like the apostle Paul, Jeremiah kept revealing facts about

---

[1] See F. J. Foakes-Jackson, *The Biblical History of the Hebrews to the Christain Era* (New York: Geo. H. Doran Co., 3rd ed., 1909), p. 307.

[2] This estimate does not include the book of Lamentations, which Jeremiah seems not to have written.

his own personality and career. In the latter part of the seventh century before Christ a lad was born in a village northeast of Jerusalem. His father served as a priest, and probably became prominent. Jeremiah says that from his birth the Lord had set him apart for the prophetic office. Scarcely had he become a man before he took up that life-work. He appears to have begun prophesying in the thirteenth year of King Josiah, and to have continued in Judah almost forty years.

Never did a nation stand more in need of a prophet. Like twin leeches idolatry and vice had kept sapping the lifeblood of Judah. No longer could she stand alone among the powers of earth. So she looked for support from Egypt or Babylon, the two empires then competing for mastery of the world. God did not will that His chosen people should receive succor from the land of the Nile. Through Isaiah He had sounded repeated warnings against entangling alliances with Egypt. Later through Jeremiah the Lord set up still other danger signals. He did not wish Judah to confide in a land that had often cast over her a spell like that of Cleopatra over Anthony.

For twoscore years as a statesman in the Kingdom of God, Jeremiah strove to keep the rulers of Judah from the clutches of Egypt, the waning power to the South. Like Evangelist in *Pilgrim's Progress* the prophet tried to persuade the people to forsake their sins and find peace with God. He sought to lead both priests and prophets to stop smiling on idolatry and vice, and re-establish the worship of God, with the religion of righteousness. He combatted the wiles of kings and nobles who would seduce the people from the grand old simplicities of God. Who can wonder that Jeremiah met with hatred and persecution?

From every outward point of view the prophet failed. Throughout those forty years he had known that he would fail. As long as Josiah sat on the throne, the prophetic reformer had the support of the king. The two men strove to carry out the teachings in the Book of the Law, which had been discovered during the repairs on the Temple about the time Jeremiah began to prophesy. That reformation never really got under way, and soon it lapsed. About ten years after Jeremiah began to prophesy King Josiah was slain in a battle with the Egyptians. From that time onward conditions in Judah waxed worse and worse. Throughout forty years, almost singlehanded, Jeremiah strove to keep his nation from blindly rushing on to ruin.

At last the doom fell. The hosts of Babylon besieged the Holy City, burned the Temple, and carried many of the people captive. What a spectacle for the aged seer as he drew nigh to the grave! No doubt he would have preferred to end his days amid the ruins of Jerusalem. Failing that, he would have chosen to accompany the exiles to Babylon. According to tradition he was borne down to Egypt by evil Hebrews who fled in terror. Under the

141

shadow of the pyramids he seems to have been stoned. If so, he died as he had lived, without wife or children or intimate friends. Only a lonesome saint of God! But what a saint! "Take him for all in all, [we] shall not look upon his like again."

Is this all we can learn about Jeremiah? By no means! If we study the records in the light of modern learning, we can get to know him as an intimate friend. Gradually we shall discover that the man himself bulks larger than his writings. We shall see him towering above the men of his day as one of those pyramids in Egypt towered above the sands along the Nile. Better still, we shall find him an intimate friend and guide in all concerns of the spirit. So let us turn to a number of passages in his writings and look for preaching values.[3] What can we learn from the experiences of this lonesome saint?

⋋ THE SAINT AS A NOVICE IN PREACHING (CH. 1)

A study of the opening chapter should help any young man who thinks about engaging in full-time Christian service. Like Jeremiah, every minister or missionary should feel sure about his call from God. Better still, he may learn that he was dedicated to the ministry at birth. God has a way of ratifying the faith of mother and father when they

[3] See also John E. McFadyen, "The Preacher's Use of Jeremiah," *A Guide to the Understanding of the Old Testament* (London: James Clarke and Co., 1927), pp. 181-89.

give their son into His hands for full-time service.[4] The Lord had set apart Jeremiah before he was born, or even conceived in the womb; but the lad seems not to have settled the matter himself until he became full-grown. Even then he held back. Like Moses, Gideon, and many another strong man of God, Jeremiah did not feel worthy. "I know not how to speak; for I am a child." (1:6.)

What an opening for a sermon about "God's Cure of an Inferiority Complex"! Not psychologically but biblically, show that such a feeling may arise in the heart of a man whom the Lord calls, and that hesitation may not prove sinful. Often such a "complex" troubles a lay man or woman. Any pastor can testify that the most useful lay leader of the flock may have had to overcome a feeling of inferiority. In dealing with such a "life situation," either privately or in the pulpit, do not argue or plead. Use facts about Jeremiah as materials for a case study. Put the emphasis where you find it in the chapter, not on the shortcoming of Jeremiah, but on the resources of his God.

Note what the Lord promises to do for this young man. "I shall send thee." Do not worry about where to labor. "I shall command thee what to say." Do not feel undue concern about what to preach. "Be not afraid of them, for I am with thee." Do not think too much about others, or about yourself. Rely upon God. His promise to be "with

[4] See the autobiography of Bishop Edwin Holt Hughes, *I Was Made a Minister* (New York and Nashville: Abingdon-Cokesbury Press, 1947), p. 254.

143

you" assures a sense of His presence, sympathy, and support. Look up to Him, and whisper in your heart: "Yea, all I need, in Thee to find." Note that after the Lord touched the young man's mouth he appears never again to have questioned his call from above. While he did not feel worthy, he knew that he could depend on a wisdom and a power vastly higher than his own.

How would such a "candidate" fare in one of our psychological tests? The examiner might report to the dean: "This young fellow shows a weak, clinging spirit. He displays none of the marks that strong men expect in their religious leader. Perhaps he could serve more effectively as a layman. Why subject him to the strain of speaking often in public?" Any such report would ignore one factor that bulked large in the experience of young Jeremiah; that was the grace of God. In the hands of the Lord such a sensitive soul may become strong as steel. As the Apostle later insisted, "God chose the weak things of the world, that he might put to shame the things that are strong." In the words of a woodsman, "The Lord can strike a mighty blow with a crooked stick." For a modern example study the life of D. L. Moody.

This chapter in Jeremiah will never become so well known as the one about the call of Isaiah. Even so, for every minister whose call resembled that of Isaiah, perhaps a hundred have had experiences like those of Jeremiah. When the Lord came to you personally, setting you apart for full-time service, did the seraphim fill the Temple with praises to God, and cause the foundation walls to tremble? Did He not rather speak to your heart with a "voice of gentle stillness"? Why labor the point? It matters not how the Lord makes known His will for a man's lifework. Yea, verily, but more than a few of us waited for years because we had no such thrilling experiences as those of Isaiah. Why did we never hear about the call of the unspectacular saint?

THE SAINT AS A MAN OF PRAYER (CHS. 12, 14)

Like many another saintly minister, Jeremiah seems to have excelled in prayer even more than in preaching. As with Job, whom the prophet resembled, the prayers often had to do with suffering. The saintly seer felt perplexed by the undeserved sorrows of God's children. Not only did he show boldness in speaking to men on behalf of God. Jeremiah became bolder still in approaching the mercy seat on behalf of suffering brethren. He even dared to "contend" with the Most High. The question at issue concerned the prosperity of the wicked. Instead of taking up the matter with the people in a sermon that would have suggested more doubts than it resolved, Jeremiah laid the problem before the Lord in prayer.

The answer came in a cryptic form. "If thou hast run with the footmen, and they have wearied thee, then how canst thou contend with horses? and though in a land of peace thou art secure, yet how wilt thou do in the pride of the Jordan?" (12:5.) "The pride of the Jordan" meant the densest jungle where wild beasts lurked while waiting to spring on their unsuspecting prey. In racing against horses, and in contending with wild beasts, a man needs the grace of Almighty God.

These words from the Lord to Jeremiah served as the text of the most famous sermon thus far in the present century. After what he termed "the suddenly dramatic death" of his wife, Dr. Arthur J. Gossip spoke from this text when first he dared to occupy the home pulpit. "But When Life Tumbles in, What Then?" In preaching on this haunting subject Dr. Gossip did not try to explain his text in detail. Still his message affords a moving commentary on the spirit of Jeremiah when he prayed. Toward the close the Glasgow divine told about life here below in the white light of eternity. He insisted that no child of God should stand in dread of either life or death. Obviously he followed the King James Version, where "the pride of the Jordan" appears as the "swelling," or the overflowing of waters in the time of a spring flood.

No, not death. For, standing in the roaring of the Jordan, cold to the heart with its dreadful chill, and very conscious of the terror of its rushing, I too, like Hopeful, can call back to you who one day in your turn will have to cross it, "Be of

146

good cheer, my brother, for I feel the bottom, and it is sound." [5]

More than one portion of Jeremiah's prayers may lead to a sermon by a pastor today. If the man in the pulpit knows the Lord, and knows how to pray, no other messages to believers will prove more helpful than ones about prayer. In Richmond, Virginia, Dr. Theodore F. Adams, of the First Baptist Church, has learned this lesson by enlisting the help of his people. Every year in June he asks them to vote on which two of the year's sermons they wish him to repeat, one from the Sunday morning service and the other from the evening. He reports that year after year one of the two chosen sermons has had to do with prayer, and sometimes both. He must know how to pray, and how to prepare a popular biblical exposition, not merely an exhortation or an expostulation. "Lord, teach us to pray!"

THE SAINT AS A MASTER OF DOCTRINE (CHS. 18–19)

Now we turn to Jeremiah's teaching about the Divine Potter. Since we shall think later about the will of God for the nation, we may consider this doctrine as it concerns only one person, like the friend in the pew. The truth before us has become known as "The Sovereignty of God," a term that meant much to people in other days, especially

[5] See *The Hero in Thy Soul* (New York: Charles Scribner's Sons, 1929), p. 116; also Hugh Black, *Listening to God* (New York: Fleming H. Revell Co., 1906), "The Heroism of Endurance," pp. 177-87.

147

when they had the right sort of king. Today we ought to employ some other phrase, because many people do not take kindly to the idea of a sovereign. Neither do they know much about a pottery. All of them ought to become concerned about "God as a Master Workman." In the passage note the appeal to imagination.

In more than a few respects the ways of a potter now resemble those in the days of Jeremiah. In England, for instance, men still speak of such a workshop as "the house of the potter." Without stretching the figure too far we may think of the local church as a pottery. Why does the home church exist if not to engage in the making of men and women, one by one, according to the plans of God? The analogy holds true also concerning the minister or missionary, who strives to mold the right sort of manhood. In our passage, however, God serves as the Potter, with human nature as the clay.

In order to mold the whirling clay the potter uses a wheel, which may correspond to the circumstances of a man's life. The potter controls the wheel so as to fashion a vessel according to his will. Some such idea dominates the poem of Robert Browning, "Rabbi Ben Ezra." In seven of the thirty-two stanzas the bard sings about God as the Potter. At the risk of marring the poem as a whole let us single out a few lines about the Potter:

> Praise be thine!
I see the whole design,

I, who saw power, see now love perfect too:
Perfect I call thy plan:
Thanks that I was a man!
Maker, remake, complete—I trust what thou shalt do!

.   .   .   .

So, take and use thy work:
Amend what flaws may lurk,
What strain o' the stuff, what warpings past the aim!
My times be in thy hand!
Perfect the cup as planned!
Let age approve of youth, and death complete the same!

Browning hints at a fact that Jeremiah stresses. A vessel may become marred in the hands of the potter. That calls for remaking, perhaps according to another pattern. Sometimes, alas, the marring may have proceeded too far. Then the vessel goes on the scrap heap. When Judas betrayed his Lord, and later threw at the rulers' feet the price of blood, they used that money to purchase a potter's field. There among the scraps of broken vessels every passer-by could think of Judas as a vessel marred in the making, through no fault of the Divine Potter.[6] No one figure can convey the whole truth about God in His dealings with men. These words about the Divine Potter tell much that we of today ought to know and heed.

[6] See William E. Hocking, *Human Nature and Its Remaking* (New Haven: Yale University Press, 1923).

The Saint as a Lover of Country (Ch. 26)

Jeremiah also excelled as a counselor of kings. After the death of Josiah the prophet seems never to have prevailed on a ruler to accept the wisdom of God. Still Jeremiah had the satisfaction of living on until everyone wished that the kings had followed his counsels. Meanwhile he stood out in many eyes as an isolationist, an obstructionist, if not a traitor. Even in our own times he has appeared as *The Rebel Prophet*.[7] Under this title a Scottish author protests that Jeremiah "still groans under misrepresentations which amount almost to libel. His spirit cries aloud for a vindicator." As Milton would say, it "appeals from tyranny to God."

Jeremiah's offense consisted in applying religion to politics. Like Amos and Isaiah, the seventh-century seer demanded from the nation righteousness, and in lieu of that he foretold coming judgment. "Is not my word like fire, saith the Lord; and like a hammer that breaketh the rock in pieces?" (23:29.) Such a reformer becomes known as an iconoclast. No wonder Jeremiah aroused the hatred and fury of leaders like those who later hounded Christ to His Cross.

In the midst of all his warnings Jeremiah also held out promises of hope. This twofold emphasis appears in his teaching about the good figs and the bad (24:1-10). He

[7] By T. Crouther Gordon (New York: Harper & Bros., 1932), p. 5.

pointed to some people in exile as good figs that God would bless, and to others who tarried in the homeland as "very bad figs, which could not be eaten, they were so bad." He also wrote for friends in exile words of wisdom that may have prevented those "displaced persons" from becoming like the "lost tribes" of the Northern Kingdom, which never returned from Captivity. Jeremiah encouraged his friends in exile to take wives, rear children, and become parts of the new community. "Seek the peace of the city whither I have caused you to be carried away captive, and pray unto the Lord for it; for in the peace thereof shall ye have peace." (29:7.)

As we have already seen more than once, many parts of the earth today need to hear such a "Gospel for Displaced Persons." During the past decade more millions have moved from former abodes than in any other period of history. Even in our own land, without direct ravages of war, statisticians compute that 40 per cent of our people have moved since the day of Pearl Harbor. Many of them have failed to get their roots firmly embedded in unfamiliar soil. Long before now they ought to have heard counsel like that of the prophet.

History has confirmed the wisdom of Jeremiah's political philosophy, and history provides "the acid test of statesmanship." "By this test the man of Anathoth is the supreme statesman of his day. . . . The true statesman is he who, like Jeremiah, has a policy for the nation, built upon high moral principles; who calls upon men to carry it out, and who, when the men fail him, summons a religion that fashions nobler men, and in the last resort calls forth a God that is equal to every emergency."

The prophet would have ascribed all of this wisdom to the leading of the Holy Spirit. As a statesman of God he knew that "politics cannot be separated from morality, and morality cannot be separated from religion." He saw too that "the central problem is the individual, and the individual is his true self only in the sight of God." [8] This does not mean that the Church or the minister should dictate to rulers and lawmakers in detail, but that the representatives of God should call for the decision of every important matter on the basis of religion and morality, rather than self-interest and expediency. This latter pathway leads to ruin.

THE SAINT AS A PROPHET OF HOPE (CHS. 31–33)

Jeremiah a prophet of hope? That sounds strange! Usually we have looked down on him as the gloomiest of pessimists. Mistakenly we have ascribed to him the doleful book of Lamentations. Often we speak of a "jeremiad," which means "a tale of sorrow, disappointment, complaint; a doleful story; a dolorous tirade." When we turn to the writings of Jeremiah, we find there one of the most

[8] Various excerpts from T. Crouther Gordon, *op. cit.*, pp. 70, 87.

glorious expressions of prophetic optimism. It shines all the more brightly because of the somber background.

"This is the covenant that I will make with the house of Israel after those days, saith the Lord. I will put my law in their inward parts, and in their hearts will I write it; and I will be their God, and they shall be my people." (31: 33.) These words point directly to our New Testament. In fact, the word "testament" literally means covenant. When we use words accurately, we speak of the Bible in two parts, the Old Covenant and the New. The Old we count good because it has come from God. The New we hold more precious because it tells more about God in Christ. The New could not have come into being without the Old. Among the prophetic writers no one saw this truth so clearly as Jeremiah, just as no New Testament author stated it so boldly as the Apostle to the Hebrews (1:1-2a).

Both in the Old Testament and in the New this idea of the covenant lies at the heart of our religion. For instance, whenever the minister stands at the Lord's Table he uses as a vital part of the Communion service the words of our Redeemer: "This cup is the new covenant in my blood." That sounds like more than an echo of Jeremiah's prediction. What, then, do we Christians understand by the word "covenant"? The answer may come from George Adam Smith:

The covenant was not a contract or bargain but an approach by God to His people, an offer of His Grace, a statement of His Will and accompanied by manifestations of His Power to redeem. . . . [This] prophecy of Christianity has hardly its equal in the Old Testament. It is the Covenant which Jesus Christ the Son of God accepted for Himself and all men and sealed with his own blood.[9]

The idea of the covenant grew out of love, rather than law. On the human level our nearest approach comes in the ceremony of marriage. At a climactic stage in one ritual the minister leads first the man and then the woman to address the other: "I do promise and covenant." Covenant to be loving and kind; to remain faithful and true. If we lift such imagery out of the human into the heavenlies, we can behold a portion of what Jeremiah and his Lord wish us to know about the New Covenant.

The New Covenant, like the Old, begins with God. He makes it, and He carries it out. He wishes it to live and work until time on earth shall end. He also made the Old Covenant, and that for a childlike people. In Jeremiah's day the Old Covenant had almost run its course. It all centered round Jerusalem, and that city had become a captive. The Old Covenant related to the Temple, and the Temple had fallen into ruins. That Covenant had to do with the Holy Land, and during the Exile most of the

[9] See *Jeremiah*, The Baird Lecture (New York: George H. Doran Co., 1923), pp. 377, 380.

people no longer dwelt in Palestine. What had they left? Little save their God and His promise of the New Covenant.

The Lord intended the New to supplant the Old. Through Moses His servant God had made the Old Covenant with the people as a whole, and had phrased it largely in terms of law. In days to come, said Jeremiah, He would make the New Covenant with His people, one by one, and that in terms of love. Instead of letting it operate chiefly in one place and for one people, He would open the gates of mercy to all the children of men, one by one. Herein lies the hope for Christian evangelism and missions.

Here too lies much of the difference between the Protestant and the Roman Catholic churches. We should not quarrel with our Catholic neighbors, or imagine that we Protestants have attained perfection. Neither should we forget why the fathers came out from the Roman Church, and what they recaptured in the way of New Covenant Christianity. Without closing our eyes to other aspects of the Reformation, let us give thanks that we live under the New Covenant. For example, think of our doctrine, the priesthood of believers, over against Roman adherence to the hierarchy. When we so believe, we take our stand with Jeremiah, with Paul, and with their Lord. God forbid that we should ever forfeit the covenant heritage we owe in large measure to Jeremiah, the Protestant saint before Christ.

For a parallel to the prophet turn to Savonarola, who preached in Florence at the time when Columbus discovered America. Just before the Reformation broke out in Germany, Savonarola attracted throngs to the cathedral. Like Jeremiah this other spokesman for God denounced the rulers and the priests. In 1498 they hounded him to death by hanging, and then they burned his body, but they could not do away with his spirit and his teachings. Not long before he went to the scaffold Savonarola said to the people:

If you ask me in general as to the issue of this struggle, I answer, "Death!" The Master, when he had used a hammer, throws it away. So He did with Jeremiah, whom He permitted to be stoned at the end of his ministry. But Rome will never put out this fire, and if it be put out, God will light another. Indeed it is already lighted everywhere, only we perceive it not.

We may find it easier to draw a parallel between Jeremiah and his coming Lord. Some of our fathers would have spoken of the prophet as a type of Christ, but we should use that term only when we have a clear warrant from the New Testament. Why not simply draw the analogy? Like our Saviour, Jeremiah was sanctified for the ministry from his mother's womb. Although he loved the joys of home, he lived unmarried. In mature years he became a "man of sorrows, and acquainted with grief." In

Jeremiah as in his Lord the man loomed far larger than the message. Unlike Isaiah, this later prophet spoke but little about the coming Messiah. In life and action, rather than in speech and writing, he did much to make ready for the advent of the King. "Beyond any other in the Old Testament, [he] was the forerunner of Jesus Christ, both in his teachings and in his personal experience." [10]

Like Hosea and other prophets Jeremiah had compassion for those who suffered. He went further; he even dared to sympathize with God. When the prophet wept, as he did at times, he shed tears because the people did not know and love their God. "He so identified himself with his people as to feel their sins and sufferings his own, and bear them on his heart before God." Even so, Jeremiah could not save those people from their sins and their judgment. He could only foreshadow the coming of One who would redeem. For many such reasons George Matheson spoke of Jeremiah as "closer to the spirit of Christ than any pre-Christian I know."

THE ADVICE OF A MASTER PREACHER

The book of Jeremiah abounds in preaching values for our day. More than a few lie about on the surface; many more lie hidden from view. There they will remain unless a man learns how to dig. Digging into this vein of rich ore

[10] See George Adam Smith, *Modern Criticism and the Preaching of the Old Testament* (New York: A. C. Armstrong and Son, 1901), p. 113.

may prove difficult for anyone, and almost impossible for a novice. Such a viewpoint appears in a letter from a pastor with years of experience as a popular interpreter of Scripture, Dr. Frank Fitt, of Memorial Presbyterian Church, Grosse Point, Michigan. After he had spent months in preparation, he gave a series of sermons leading up to the Advent season, under the heading, "The Message of Jeremiah for Today." In most cases he stressed doctrine:

> True Religion Not External
> God Works Through Individuals
> The Divine Potter Will Prevail
> Tragedy Can Enlarge Our Vision
> God Can Transform Our Lives
> Prayer as Fellowship with God
> Loyalty to God Comes First
> We Must Never Surrender Hope
> Faith Defies the Impossible

The pastor enjoyed that series, and so did the people. Afterward he wrote about the difficulty of preaching from the book of Jeremiah: "It requires not merely a knowledge of the Bible book but also a knowledge of life today. The latter factor causes trouble for most of us. A young minister would need to be a genius to express what only a long and faithful experience on the pastoral side can give a man." To all of which one can only say, "Amen!"

The young preacher should not embark at once on a

tour through the book of Jeremiah. He should live with it for a number of years, and also live with God's people. Little by little he will come to know the hearts of men, and gain skill enough to interpret the writings of the prophet whom he has learned to love and revere as one of the most Christlike saints in the Old Testament. When at last he embarks on that series, he will find in it both power and joy.

CHAPTER VIII

Habakkuk

THE CONVERSION OF AN HONEST DOUBTER

No Old Testament book . . . is able to do more for the burdened souls of men or raise them to higher levels of hope and confidence than the brief prophecy of Habakkuk. Yet it is one of the least understood and most neglected of Bible books. We need to recover a true knowledge of it, to read it, love it, use it. For if ever the message of this inspired book was needed, it is needed today.[1]

IN THE DAYS OF HABAKKUK THE PEOPLE SORELY NEEDED a prophet of assurance and hope. This contemporary of Jeremiah saw conditions in Judah growing worse and worse. Writing about 600 B.C., or a little earlier, Habakkuk faced oncoming exile. He also met a rising tide of doubt, even among the noblest saints. Speaking out of his own experience he dealt with those doubts at their source. He wrote in a fashion all his own, with much of beauty and power.

This little book tells practically all we know about Habakkuk. His name comes from a Hebrew root that

[1] Raymond Calkins, *The Modern Message of the Minor Prophets* (New York: Harper & Bros., 1947), p. 92.

160

means to caress or embrace. According to Martin Luther this Hebrew prophet served as a "heartener." On the basis of his own struggles with doubt, and his own victory through faith, he put heart into people who might otherwise have yielded to despair. Anyone who knows *The American Mind* [2] today, or the mind of our globe, can sense the timeliness of this little book by Habakkuk, as great as it is small.

The prophecy falls into three parts, corresponding to the chapters in our English Bible. In the first main part Habakkuk sets forth the problem, which has to do with God. At a time when the wicked prosper and the righteous do not, how can anyone keep on believing in God? The second chapter gives part of the answer, which comes from the watchtower of faith. The third chapter soars into a declaration of faith and hope, with power to uplift. "Search the Scriptures through," says Dr. Calkins, "and you will find nothing so matchless in concentrated power." These three parts may lead to that many "chapter sermons," with others on separate verses in their background.

A Man Wrestling with Doubt, or a Doubter's Dialogue with God (Ch. 1)

Note here the problem approach, which sometimes appears among us as a modern discovery. Note also the stress

[2] Under this title by Henry S. Commager see an able "Interpretation of American Life and Character Since the 1880's" (New Haven: Yale University Press, 1950); especially Ch. IX, "Religious Thought and Practice."

on one man as a doubter. Why preach about *The Gospel for an Age of Doubt*,[3] when the Bible throws the spotlight on one person? So does the hymn by George Croly:

> Teach me the struggles of the soul to bear,
> To check the rising doubt, the rebel sigh.

In like manner Browning and Tennyson often deal with doubt as it concerns one man alone with his Lord. Why do we in the pulpit often deal with doubt in the plural, or else impersonally?

"Bring your doubts to God and seek His grace in conquering them one by one." So the interpreter might plead today. Then the hearer could respond with Habakkuk: "My doubts have to do with God Himself!" Very well, bring them straight to Him. The prophet did so, and in light from above he found both peace and joy. So will any other honest doubter who perseveres in dealing with God. In quest of light he may receive from Habakkuk more encouragement than from any other Bible doubter, such as John the Baptist or Thomas, not to speak of Job and the author of Ps. 73.[4] All of these have much in common, and much to contribute in our day.

[3] Under this title see a helpful book by Henry van Dyke (New York: The Macmillan Co., 1896).

[4] See Arthur S. Peake, *The Problem of Suffering in the Old Testament* (London: C. H. Kelly, 1904).

THE CONVERSION OF AN HONEST DOUBTER

The book in hand starts with the doubter's complaints against his God (1:2-4). Even to a good man's prayers why does God keep silent? In the presence of wickedness that triumphs on every side, why does not the Almighty act? Since the ungodly gloat over their evil deeds, and even drive the righteous to the wall, why does not God intervene? As Carlyle once exclaimed in a time of moral crisis, "He does nothing!" In like manner today the world around, "frail children of dust, and feeble as frail" keep crying out to God, one by one, "My God, my God, why?"

The Lord's answer (vss. 5-11) to Habakkuk's outburst contains the heart of biblical philosophy concerning doubt. "I am working in your days." "I raise up the Chaldees, that bitter and hasty nation." The Lord God proposed to use this national power as a scourge to discipline His chosen people. In a time and in a way that He did not make known to Habakkuk, God would deal with the Chaldeans in judgment. Today instead of trying to identify the "Chaldeans" in the modern age let us lay hold of the main teaching. The "Chaldeans" come, fulfill their mission, and then depart. A decade or two ago some of us would have identified a certain power as the Chaldeans, and today still another nation. About such things we may not always feel sure, but back of them we can behold

163

the hand of our God.[5] For a commentary here why not turn to a hymn that we use with the tune "Russian Hymn"?

God the All-wise! by the fire of Thy chastening
Earth shall to freedom and truth be restored;
Through the thick darkness Thy Kingdom is hastening;
Give to us peace in our time, O Lord.

At a time of honest doubt the soul can find its peace in God. Believing where he cannot see or understand, the former doubter learns to rely on the goodness of God. However little he may comprehend the workings of providence among the nations and in his own affairs, the seeker after light comes to rest in the assurance that the wisdom and power of the Almighty obey the behests of His mercy and grace. If such a working philosophy sounds strange to any devotee of science, let him give heed to Professor Henry Norris Russell of Princeton University, one of our most distinguished astronomers. A woman with more zeal than tact spoke to him as a lay officer in the home church: "How can you as a foremost scientist still believe in God?"

"Madam, that all depends on how big a God you have, and how much you trust Him. Can you believe in Him despite changing ideas about details?"

[5] See also in James Black, *Days of My Autumn* (London: Hodder and Stoughton, 1950), pp. 89-100, a striking sermon, "The Man Who Made the Earth to Tremble."

Why not preach the substance of this opening chapter in Habakkuk? If so, take for granted that many a strong man today has doubts. So has many a conscientious woman. According to church workers in university centers, young women entertain as many doubts as their brothers, and sometimes the young women suffer silently. In all sorts of subtle ways the doubts of today may differ from those of yesterday, but from age to age they all have to do with God. For example in one of her best novels about Virginia, *The Sheltered Life*, Ellen Glasgow has a character explain: "I am a Victorian at heart. Even when the Victorians doubted the existence of God, they still believed in His goodness." Today, with more than a few, doubts concern His character. In the home parish what are you doing to help the honest doubter? For a text why not use this one from Habakkuk—"Thou that art of purer eyes than to behold evil" (1:13)?

A WATCHTOWER OF FAITH (CH. 2)

From a watchtower the guardian of a community can see the approach of an enemy, and sound the alarm. The man on the tower must know how to catch the attention of those who rush swiftly by. What a figure for the work of the pastor today, when most men become distracted! The poet Habakkuk had a message for his day: "The just shall live by his faith" (2:4*b* King James Version). More literally, "the righteous man shall live by his faithfulness,"

165

or loyalty. These words helped Paul in setting men free from bondage to the law, and Luther in delivering Protestants from serfdom of another kind. To Paul and Luther the text meant the sort of faith that saves. To us the words may also speak about the kind of faith that serves. Both Luther and Paul would agree with Habakkuk that nothing on earth reaches closer to heaven than loyalty to God. A subject for the sermon, "A Man's Loyalty to His God."

By way of contrast the singer on the watchtower of faith utters five "taunt songs" in which he sets forth the difficulties of unbelief. If the man who believes must face problems, so must the one who disbelieves. Since everyone must serve some person or cause outside himself, what else can anyone put in the place of God? The answers from the prophet may differ from those of doubters today. If so, why not substitute a few of those other alternatives? Then see how loyalty to God proves better by far than any or all man-made substitutes. Habakkuk here uses a case method, with hypothetical examples something like those of Phillips Brooks. In each case, as with Brooks, one man serves as an object lesson.

The first case (vss. 6b-8) has to do with a man's worship of power as his god; the second (9-11), with the one who lives in order to build a house; the third (12-14), with the tyrant who establishes a city by shedding blood; the fourth (15-17), with the devotee of strong drink and all its attendant sirens; the fifth (18-20), with the victim of

166

idolatry. This last word picture led to a recent sermon about the folly of worshiping what we manufacture. Why deal with the matter in the plural? Habakkuk, like his coming Lord, pointed to one man, strangely like that friend yonder in the pew.

In the midst of these taunt songs the prophet strikes off a number of sayings that call for sermons. "The earth shall be filled with the knowledge of the glory of the Lord, as the waters cover the sea." (2:14.) "A Vision of the World Transformed." Here the prophet looks out over the nations with all their folly. Then he sets forth the glory of a world in which God will have His way. The text calls for a message about world missions, with stress on the power of the gospel to transform. In order to do so it needs to become known through preaching and teaching by many a man like Habakkuk.

"Woe unto him that giveth his neighbor drink." (2:15a.) "The Peril in Social Drinking." Here again the stress falls on a single person, the one who tempts another. The tempter may pride himself on being able to control his appetite, but why should he expose a weaker brother to peril? If a minister does not devote an entire sermon to the subject, at least he can make clear the sin of encouraging anyone else to drink. Why should not every man abstain, if only for the sake of his neighbor?

"The Lord is in his holy temple: let all the earth keep silence before him." (2:20.) "The Meaning of Our Worship." After showing the folly of an idolater, Habakkuk sounds "A Call to Public Worship." To this hour the minister can find no better words with which to open his part of morning worship. Better still, he can preach about this text, with its "two contrasting truths" which must have delighted the soul of F. W. Robertson. First, the presence of God in the sanctuary. Second, the response of His children everywhere. Public worship means God's way of revealing Himself in grace, and our way of responding to Him in faith. Unlike other golden texts in Habakkuk, this one has to do with the plural. It calls for a sermon about corporate worship. If a minister wishes to preach about God's revelation to one man, and about his response, the text may come from Isa. 6. Deal with one passage or the other, and not with both at once. People have become confused by our hop-skip-and-jump methods of preaching from the Bible.

AN OPTIMIST AT WORSHIP (CH. 3)

Following the call for adoration comes an entire chapter about worship. Here the prophet speaks for himself as once a doubter. In terms of our day the chapter consists of a prayer, a hymn, and a creed. The prayer and the creed lend themselves to the uses of the modern pulpit. The song that intervenes (3:3-15) may prove difficult to make clear and luminous. It all has to do with God, and that in action. Seldom even in Job or Isaiah does Holy Writ present more

168

of grandeur and of glory about God, as He strides across the habitable earth and makes it ready for the dwelling of the Redeemer. All this the minister should know and feel. Still he ought to think twice before he ventures into the pulpit with a sermon about this song in Habakkuk.

"Revive thy work in the midst of the years." (3:2b.) In clarity the opening prayer stands out by contrast with the hymn. The prayer calls for a message with the same sort of clearness and quiet beauty. "A Prayer for Revival." This text once supplied the motif for a strong book by Charles G. Finney, *Lectures on Revivals of Religion*. Opinions may differ about "revivalism" in the United States, but no one can fail to see that revivals of another sort occupied a large place in Bible days, and in the later history of the Church. Since no one has discovered any other adequate name for the quickening of God's children and the restoration of spiritual life to the Church, why not retain the word revival, and cleanse it from American excrescences? Away with our former emphasis on money and machinery and mob psychology! With Habakkuk let us pray and long for the sort of revival that comes from God.[6]

The noblest words in the book (3:17-18) contain "The Creed of an Optimist." The paragraph includes two additional verses, one preceding and one following, but the

---

[6] For a series of object lessons, study the movement in 1857-58, the best of our revivals. It began with laymen at prayer.

two in the center provide more than enough ideas for a sermon. If anyone tried to deal with all four verses, he might get lost in detail and become obscure, or else dull. In popular exposition, effectiveness depends largely on willingness to select and omit. Only one large message for each sermon!

In terms of a farmstead Habakkuk sings about belief in God despite the failure of all the things on which a farmer depends. These two verses show how to use concrete facts in making clear an abiding principle. Behold the fig tree, the vine, the olive, and the harvest field—all of them bare. Also behold the fold without a flock, and the stalls without an ox. Like Job, after the storm had swept away his wealth of worldly goods, this farmer looks out over empty stables and barren fields. A few months ago he had in view everything heart could desire. Now he has nothing, nothing except his God! This little scene in Habakkuk deserves to become as well known as the opening chapter in the book of Job.

Once a group of friends conversed with Daniel Webster about the noblest piece of literature in the English Bible. One man spoke about the Genesis account of the creation; another, about the Sermon on the Mount; a third, about a part of the Apocalypse, with its description of the redeemed in glory. Then Webster recited from memory, word for word, the creed of Habakkuk as given in the King James Version:

> Although the fig tree shall not blossom,
> neither shall fruit be in the vines;
> the labour of the olive shall fail,
> and the fields shall yield no meat;
> the flock shall be cut off from the fold,
> and there shall be no herd in the stalls:
> Yet I will rejoice in the Lord,
> I will joy in the God of my salvation.

"I am amazed," said Webster, "that no artist has seen here a subject for a masterpiece. Habakkuk sitting in the midst of his dreadful desolation, still praising God and rejoicing in his unseen Saviour." Why not go into the pulpit to paint that picture with words?

What a book full of suggestions for sermons to the honest doubter! The prophet begins with the problem of honest doubt as it concerns God Himself. Then the book deals with the alternatives of unbelief. At last the prophecy soars into triumphant assurance about the Lord God Omnipotent as the ground of all assurance and hope.[7] If any minister will live with this little book long enough to see it as a whole, and then in its parts, he will agree with Dr. Calkins that "no other Old Testament book is able to do more for the burdened souls of men, or raise them to higher levels of hope and confidence." When at last the minister preaches from it, the hearer will praise his God.

[7] See James S. Stewart, *The Gates of New Life* (New York: Charles Scribner's Sons, 1940), especially sermon II, "The Lord God Omnipotent Reigneth."

171

Chapter IX

Ezekiel

THE VISIONS OF A ZEALOUS CHURCHMAN

Who among us today has a good word for ezekiel and his writings? Any biblical interpreter who wishes to by-pass this long book can find encouragement from various scholars. One of them refers to Ezekiel as "the first fanatic in the Bible," and as a dogmatist whose prose at worst seems "pedantic, monotonous, and repetitious." Another learned author, less caustic, speaks of this man's work as "the most neglected of prophetic writings." As for personality, some insist that he resembles John Calvin, whom they do not admire. The present discussion assumes that the compilers of the Sacred Canon acted wisely in giving the writings of Ezekiel almost one twentieth of the entire Scriptures. Many of us today need to know these visions of a zealous churchman.

For lack of popular favor the prophet himself must bear part of the blame. He tells much about the individual with relation to God, but reveals little about Ezekiel, so little that a student today can scarcely form a mental picture. Once, however, the seer gives a personal detail that suggests much. On the evening of the day when his wife died,

172

this man preached to the people. In general he appears to have been a priest and to have prophesied twenty-two years, eleven before 586 B.C. and eleven afterward. According to some recent writers he spent all this time at Jerusalem. Most of us think of him as being carried captive to Babylon in 586 B.C. In any case that year afforded his prophet ministry a sort of dividing ridge.

The first half of the book (chs. 1–24) came from the period before the main captivity in 586 B.C. In these prophecies, mostly dark, Ezekiel uttered words of warning and rebuke. In the less gloomy half (chs. 25–48), after telling much about doom on other nations, he brought assurance and hope to the people of God as a Church. Like most generalizations, this account makes the facts appear far too simple. At least we can agree with Edgar J. Goodspeed that Ezekiel "had the very difficult duty of keeping his people true to their faith in the face of the greatest discouragement—the destruction of their nation and their worship, and apparently of their religion." [1] His book, says Robert H. Pfeiffer, marks the transition from Israel as a nation with a country and a state, to Judaism as a holy congregation within an alien empire.[2] How up-to-date that sounds! What a message for millions of those "displaced persons"! Even if we in the States do not yet suffer with them directly, we ought to know and sympathize.

[1] *How to Read the Bible* (Philadelphia: John C. Winston Co., 1946), p. 29.
[2] *Introduction to the Old Testament* (New York: Harper & Bros., 1948), p. 558, *et al.*

Unlike many theologians now, Ezekiel begins with God, not with man. According to Delitzsch the opening chapter contains "the grandest of Biblical visions," all of it about God. The imagery of the wheels may have seemed clear to people in Ezekiel's time, and to Delitzsch as a scholar of yesterday, but these ideas seem hazy to us in America now. To a scholar they speak about omnipresence and omniscience, omnipotence and transcendence. To the popular interpreter these images ought to mean something in thought-forms of the man on the street: the God of all the peoples on earth, the God of all wisdom for men, the God of all power to move, the God of all right to rule. What if the Holy City has become a captive and the Temple has fallen into ruin? The glory of God does not depend on any such place or thing. He lives, and He reigns; He knows, and He cares. What a line of thought for a message from this opening verse! "I Saw Visions of God." "Abiding Facts About God."

Doctrine more immediately "practical" appears in the account of Ezekiel's call. "Son of man, stand upon thy feet, and I will speak with thee." (2:1.) "The Manliness of a Minister." These six "marks of a man" would provide too much material for a charge to a young clergyman. In fact, any one of the six might serve. (1) The man who has courage to speak the truth (2:1-7). Like John Knox such a one fears God so much that he dreads not the face of

174

anyone else. (2) The man who lives on the Bible (2:8–3:3). Literally he devours it, finding it sweet to the taste. In the words of the Book of Common Prayer, he "inwardly digests" it, and from the Bible receives strength to do the will of God. (3) The man with the flint face (3:4-11). Like the coming Christ of the Cross the prophet will not swerve from the appointed path.

(4) The man who obeys the Holy Spirit (3:12-15). In this book the Hebrew word for Spirit occurs fifty-two times, or almost one seventh of the number in the entire Old Testament. (5) The man who serves as a watchman (3:16-21). He warns both the wicked and the righteous. (6) The man who moves according to the will of God (3:22-27). "The hand of the Lord was upon me." Repeatedly this phrase appears in the book of Ezekiel. Still more often come the other words, "son of man," which mean that he identifies himself with the people of God. Under the guiding hand of the Lord behold this sympathetic friend and helper of men. Thank God for such ways of emphasis through meaningful repetition!

From now on we can merely single out passages of special interest for today. Among them all note Ezekiel's repeated emphasis on the individual. "The fathers have eaten sour grapes, and the children's teeth are set on edge." (18:2*b*.) In its own setting the parable of the sour grapes may lead to a message, "A Bible Study in Hered-

175

ity." The proverb means that when the fathers do wrong, their children must suffer. In a large sense this holds true. "The evil that men do lives after them," and most of all in their sons. Ezekiel takes for granted the power of heredity and home environment, but he insists that no son of a wicked father need despair, just as the son of a pious father must not presume. Note here the stress on the truth as it concerns one young man.

"All souls are mine," says God. "The soul that sinneth, it shall die"; that is, unless it repents and turns to God. His grace proves mightier by far than heredity and all the other human forces that affect a son's character and destiny. Under God, what a young man becomes must depend chiefly on himself and on the set of his sail. Herein lies much of the peril and the fascination of living on earth today. Within narrow limits a scientist can tell how heredity will work among roses or dogs, but no present-day Mendel or Dalton can begin to explain the moral differences between an evil father and a good son, or between an evil son and a good father. Under God that difference depends mainly on the boy. Toward the end of this chapter comes one of the most evangelical sayings in the Old Testament. "I have no pleasure in the death of him that dieth. . . . Wherefore turn yourselves, and live." (18:32.) As we have already seen, our day has heard about *Grapes of Wrath*. Why not preach about the grace of God? As in the Lord's allegory about the grapes (John 15), look on

God as the Divine Husbandman who longs to see good fruit.

Still more strongly does the prophet appeal to imagination in his lament over the city of Tyre (ch. 27). Unlike most biblical writers, this one knows the ways of the sea and of ships. He also feels at home in the geography of the ancient world, as many of us do not. At least we know that in days of old, Tyre became a commercial power, and at certain times ruled the waves of the eastern world. Because of geographical details we may not appreciate the first twenty-five verses, but we ought to admire the latter part of the chapter (vss. 26-36), with the most beautiful poetry in the entire book. As a whole the passage makes a Bible student think of chapter 27 in the book of the Acts, where Luke has written the world's most famous description of a storm at sea. In preaching about either passage do not blur the picture by attempting to explain the other. Focus attention on one scene.

In the closing words of his poem Ezekiel addresses an apostrophe to Tyre after she has vanished. Once rich and strong, haughty and disdainful of other peoples, at last she has become desolate. The poet looks on Tyre as a gallant vessel whose rowers have brought her out into mighty waters, where the east wind has broken her to pieces in the heart of the sea. Then the bard echoes wailings from the beach as loved ones mourn for men lost on the ship that will sail no more. "Who is there like Tyre, like her that is brought to silence in the midst of the sea?" (vs. 32b.) What a text for a day when big business has adopted many of the ideas that led to the downfall of Tyre! Anyone who has visited the mean little hamlet of Tyre can see the contrast between the "olden golden glory" of times bygone and the squalor of all that remains from that splendor by the sea. *Sic transit gloria mundi!*

Ezekiel does not always move on such a high level. In chapter 33 he appears as a zealous churchman rather than a poet. Here he returns to the idea of "The Watchman in God's City." These searching words should come home to every minister, and every other leader in Church or state. If the watchman sees an invading host and sounds the trumpet of alarm, he can say with the Apostle: "I am pure from the blood of all men" (Acts 20:26b). If he sees the sword coming and gives no alarm, he will have on his hands the blood of the slain. The prophet here speaks about an invading host, but his words also tell about the inroads of sin. As George Adam Smith once declared, a man may sin as much by silence when he ought to speak as by speech when he ought to keep silent.

Even the most sincere minister needs to beware. This chapter leads up to striking words about "The Perils of a Popular Preacher" (33:30-33). Strange as the fact may seem to us, Ezekiel must have attracted the people of his day.

He was a popular preacher. His sermons were among the few sensations that relieved the gray monotony of life in exile. Men talked about them as they stood at their doors. They invited each other to go and hear Ezekiel. He "was unto them as a very lonely song of one that hath a pleasant voice, and can play well on an instrument"; and he had as much religious influence. "They hear thy words," said the Lord to His people, "but they do them not." [3]

Ten hundred years later the people of Constantinople thronged to hear John Chrysostom. In more recent times the elite of France took delight in the sacred oratory of Massillon and Bourdaloue. After they have hung on the words of a pulpit orator the hearers may admire and praise his voice and gestures, his diction and personality; but do they accept and obey the word of God from his mouth? Is there not a call for such a warning now? What sort of preacher does many a congregation desire? What kind of messenger does the student of divinity wish to become? What type of pulpit master do we professors hold up as examples? Too often we laud the pulpit orator, who calls attention chiefly to himself, not to his Saviour; or the sermonizer, who directs attention to his masterpiece, not to his God. Why not give the preference to the pastoral evangelist, who puts God first, the hearer next, and self last? He knows that "the best speaking voice never is heard."

[3] See R. H. Bennett, *The Religion of the Post-Exilic Prophets* (Edinburgh: T. and T. Clark, 1907), p. 27.

Every pastor ought also to study the following chapter, about "Shepherds That Feed Themselves" (34:2). Here and often elsewhere Ezekiel follows Jeremiah in denouncing false prophets.[4] Today a minister would scarcely carry such a message into the pulpit on the Lord's Day, but he could deal with the facts at a midweek service, or in a Bible conference. Laymen as well as clergy ought to sense the importance of ministerial leadership in the Church, and of holding up biblical standards for God's undershepherds. Whenever in history the Church has needed a reformation or a revival, the fault has lain largely at the doors of the clergy. Do we not need a reformation and a revival today?

In contrast with much of the preceding gloom the thirty-sixth chapter brings out "The Gospel According to Ezekiel." Here as elsewhere he stands forth as "the first systematic theologian in the Old Testament." His words full of gospel truth originally referred to return from exile, but for us they also tell about redemption from sin. The ideas in chapter thirty-six resemble those of Paul as the foremost interpreter of Christianity, and they appear in much the same order as in the Pauline epistles, though in a form more condensed. "No passage in the Old Testament of the same extent offers so complete a parallel to New Testament doctrine, particularly to that of St. Paul. It is doubtful if the apostle ever quotes Ezekiel anywhere,

[4] For a popular account of these men see James Stalker, *The Preacher and His Models* (New York: A. and C. Armstrong, 1891), ch. IV.

but his line of thought entirely coincides." [5] Any one of the six truths that appear below would lead to a helpful message for today. As a group they include the heart of what Protestants believe about God. In each case the stress falls on Him, not on us:

The Unmerited Mercy of God (36:22-23)
The Chosen People of God (vs. 24)
The Cleansing Power of God (vs. 25)
The New Heart from God (vs. 26)
The Indwelling Spirit of God (vs. 27)
The Loyal People of God (vs. 28)

Much more appeal to imagination comes through Ezekiel's vision in the valley full of bones, many and dry (ch. 37). Behold a valley in which two armies have fought to a standstill, until at last both have slunk away by night, leaving their dead to bury the dead. In time the valley has become strewn with bones. To Ezekiel's friends the valley may have stood for the exile. To us the vision tells about a field for evangelism at home or missions abroad. The valley full of dry bones leads us to envision vast stretches of earth without God and without hope for this world or the next. More simply, these dry bones symbolize dead souls.

In this valley of vision the man of God surveys hosts of dead men's bones (vss. 1-3). Under the guiding hand

[5] See A. B. Davidson, *The Book of the Prophet Ezekiel* in the "Cambridge Bible Series" (Cambridge: The University Press, 1906), p. 266.

181

of his Lord the prophet moves about among the bones, until he hears a voice from above, with a question that ought to echo in the soul of every preacher today: "Son of man, can these bones live?" "Man in the pulpit, have you a gospel for dead souls? Do you believe in miracles today? Do you feel sure that God can still bring life from the dead?" For an object lesson of such a believer, read the life of Richard Baxter in Kidderminster parish, or of Mary Slessor among African natives.

In Ezekiel's vision, marvel of marvels, hear him preaching to dry bones (vss. 4-8). "Ye shall live; and ye shall know that I am the Lord." These last words form another of the prophet's recurrent refrains. He wants everyone to know God as the Lord of life. After the herald utters these words of hope, bones come together with bones and become bodies of men, but without any breath. Only a vision, but what does it mean? It may tell us about the transformation that the preaching of the gospel has made in China and India, in Africa and the South Pacific. "These that have turned the world upside down are come hither also." Commotion, upheaval, and outward change—all from God, but yet not enough. Those bodies in the valley of vision still lie dead. So do countless souls today the world around, for in the Scriptures death in a soul means separation from God.

So the vision moves on to its climax (vss. 9-10). "Prophesy unto the wind." In terms of our time, pray for the

Spirit! In the Hebrew, as in the Greek, the word for wind also serves for spirit. Symbolically this part of the vision declares that after the preacher has done all he can accomplish as a herald, there remains vastly more that only God can do by His Spirit. He alone can impart life to the dead. In terms of today He only can lead sinners to know God as Father, so as to find in Him life everlasting, beginning here and now.

The three stages of the vision mark increasing importance. First, the presence of the seer in the midst of the valley shows that the minister ought to move among men who most need the gospel. Second, in preaching to the unsaved and unchurched a man ought to utter a message of assurance and hope. "Ye shall live; and ye shall know." Third, he ought to pray for the Spirit to enter lifeless souls and do what all the men on earth can never hope to accomplish. Life from the dead, with newborn souls ready for service in the army of the King! What does every community the world around need so much today as this gospel of life from the dead?

Why have three parts in such a teaching message, rather than two or four? Indeed, why have any divisions at all? In feeding his flock out of the Book, why did Alexander Maclaren often use "a three-pronged fork"? We older men sometimes overdo such a use of divisions; too often we have three; but we feel that younger men should learn to preach this way at times. When a teaching minister finds in his passage three large truths for today, and only three, why should he not call attention to the threefold structure of his passage? Not every part of Holy Writ lends itself to this kind of interpretation, but the vision in the valley of dry bones presents three stages that stand out. So does the vision to which we now turn. In dealing with a passage in the Bible a man who uses imagination sees what God has caused to be written. The pulpiteer who relies on fancy may try to invent where he ought rather to discover, interpret, and illuminate.[6]

In the forty-seventh chapter the vision calls for a sermon about world missions. "World Missions in the Old Testament." Just before the sermon let the people stand to sing a familiar hymn, "The Morning Light Is Breaking." After they sit down, have the choir sing softly, without announcement or accompaniment, the stanza about the "blest river of salvation." Then the opening words from the pulpit may call attention to the fact that this missionary hymn comes out of the Bible. Get the hearer to see that in the Holy Land the river flows through terrain almost devoid of water. Before starting to prepare this sermon a man ought to study with care the geography of the Holy City and of the region down to the Dead Sea. The facts about the Holy Land represent truths about the Kingdom as they appeal to the eye of the soul. Before anyone tries to in-

[6] See my *Preaching from the Bible,* ch. XII, "The Interpreter's Imagination," a discussion that owes much to Wordsworth, Coleridge, and John L. Lowes.

terpret the facts figuratively he should understand them geographically.

The first stage of the vision (47:1-2) tells about the source of God's river. In the resulting sermon never let the friend in the pew lose sight of that river and that source. A well-known author has written a whole book about the Christian religion in terms of a river that comes from God. The stream now in view flows out from beneath the eastern side of the temple area. In all Jerusalem and its environs a visitor can find only one source of water —the Virgin's Fountain, which Ezekiel must have had in mind. Symbolically he means that the "blest river of salvation" has its source in God, and that it flows out from the Church. What a message from our zealous churchman!

The next part of the vision (vss.3-5) tells about the deepening and broadening of the life-giving stream. Nothing of the sort has ever appeared in geography or in nature. Without any other source of supply for its waters, how could a river grow deeper and broader? Indeed, if a stream flowed through such terrain without losing any of its precious waters, that would seem wondrous. How does this one increase with its onward flow? Only by the grace of God, in the form of a miracle. By way of translating this imagery into modern terms the late Robert E. Speer used often to quote from Adolf Harnack, master historian who wrote *The Expansion of Christianity in the*

First Three Centuries.[7] Today one can find the same facts, more in detail and without the thrill, in K. S. Latourette's work, *A History of the Expansion of Christianity.*[8]

How can anyone account for such an expansion of the Early Church? Only on the basis of what some of us term the Supernatural. The same holds true in the last stage of our vision (vss. 6-12), which has to do with the influence of the river. What mean the trees that spring up along the banks of the stream? If the semidesert land represents the aridness of a region without God, the trees must tell of the change that comes over the lives of men when they respond to the healing streams of God's grace. Since a hymn at its best means doctrine set to music, let this truth come out of a missionary song that we all love:

> Hail to the brightness of Zion's glad morning,
>> Long by the prophets of Israel foretold. . . .
> Lo, in the desert rich flowers are springing,
>> Streams ever copious are flowing along.

Those waters still keep flowing. In time they will transform the Dead Sea so as to make it the abode of life and beauty. Here let the Dead Sea stand for all that the world, the flesh, and the Devil can do to curse God's "good earth." Since the Dead Sea has no outlet, the longer it re-

[7] Two volumes, transl. (New York: G. P. Putnam's Sons, 1905).

[8] Seven volumes (New York: Harper & Bros., 1937-45), a masterpiece of erudition, and an unfailing source of facts for sermons.

mains inert the more it must abound in filth, as the scum and offscouring of creation. In recent years men have begun to find in the Dead Sea all sorts of hidden treasure, but that line of thought would call for another sermon, different from this one based on Ezekiel.

As an example of the gospel's power to transform, look at one of the Melanesian Islands in the South Pacific.[9] If you could have gone to that island a hundred years ago you would have suffered at the hands of cannibals who took delight in unspeakable filth. In that lone island, without a large population, murders used to number one or two hundred a year, and in countless other ways life did not seem worth living. During the past sixty years, the present chief declares, he has not known of a single murder. He reports no jails, no drunkenness, no social diseases, at least none among the natives. If you could ask him about the secret of such a transformation, the aged believer would tell you with joy, "Jesus Christ and His Gospel!" If you inquired of some other native, more childlike, he would point to the missionary and exclaim, "Massa blong Jesu Christ!" Then he would turn to the missionary's wife, "Missa blong Jesu Christ!" What an up-to-the-minute version of the Gospel According to Ezekiel!

So much for a few of many preaching values in this prophetic book that the Church of today neglects. We

[9] See also H. P. Van Dusen, *They Found the Church There* (New York: Charles Scribner's Sons, 1945).

have gone into it far enough to make clear that Ezekiel stands ready to bring light and leading for any minister or congregation. If some portions of the book seem obscure and even fantastic, do not blame Ezekiel, but seek for the illumination that comes through waiting on the Lord in the spirit of prayer. As the Spirit shines upon the open page and brings to light one glorious truth after another, share with the people these visions that have made your own heart burn with new zeal for the Church. By way of encouragement for mastery of the book, think about the following truths it stands ready to teach:

1. *The Importance of Biblical Doctrine.* Since our times call for more of a popular teaching ministry, why not prepare to meet this need? You can do so in large measure out of this book. Be sure that you translate Ezekiel's imagery into thought-forms of our day. His ways of setting forth truth may not fit our time any better than our ways of speech would have seemed clear and luminous to his friends in Babylon. To preach doctrine and duty today means to interpret God and His revealed will in terms that the hearer knows and likes.

2. *The Priority of God.* In theology, as in life, we of today tend to give the Almighty a secondary place, or even a tertiary. For example, in dealing with a passage about God, why does an up-to-date minister not begin about Him? Sometimes, for the sake of interest perhaps he may not, but somehow he should make clear that God in

188

Christ looms larger than all things else on earth and in heaven.

3. *The Spirit of Judaism.* "All that has been persistent and fundamental in the Judaism of twenty centuries can be traced back to Ezekiel. He is the father of the Jewish Church.[10] To a lesser degree that statement would hold true of the Roman Catholic Church. In a day when we seek to understand both Jews and Catholics we should know the book of Ezekiel.

4. *The Centrality of the Church.* In various circles of life we American Protestants have tended toward individualism. Some of us formerly stressed the right of private judgment so strongly that we tended to minimize the central importance of the Church in the mystery of redemtpion. Today we are beginning to rediscover the Church. Should we not also resolve to know this book that exalts the Church?

5. *The Work of the Ministry.* More than any other prophet, more even than Jeremiah, this later seer holds up lofty standards for the minister. Like John Henry Jowett in *The Preacher, His Life and Work*, Ezekiel thinks and speaks in terms of one man as typical of many. His book should lead us to loftier ideals about the minister of today and tomorrow. Does the local interpreter, like Ezekiel,

[10] See William F. Lofthouse, *The Prophet of Reconstruction* (New York: Frowde, 1920), p. 21.

189

know how to gain and hold attention without resorting to wisecracks and even to buffoonery?

6. *The Rights of the Individual*. In a broad sense the Old Testament stresses the Church and the state, whereas the New emphasizes the individual. In many places, however, the reverse holds true. In this respect, as in others, Ezekiel stands between the Old and the New. He would have us look on the individual as a vital part of the corporate Church. What a lesson for our day in the homeland and across the seven seas. "A man's a man for a' that."

7. *The Call for Evangelism*. While not himself an evangelist in the New Testament sense of the term, Ezekiel prepared the way for presenting the gospel to the unsaved and unchurched here at home.

8. *The Cause of World Missions*. Although not himself a world missionary in our sense of the word, this man held up ideals that ought to send the Church out to capture the world for Christ.

9. *The Importance of Apocalyptic Writings*. Some of Ezekiel's glowing promises yet await fulfillment. Not only did his writings influence the book of Revelation. The two works together, amid all their difficulties of interpretation, show the importance of what lies beyond the present age. God grant that in the light of Ezekiel and the Apocalypse the unknown future may become more largely a mystery full of radiance!

CHAPTER X

THE MINE FOR THE PREACHER TODAY

IN A TYPICAL PARISH TODAY THE TIME HAS COME FOR more of a popular teaching ministry. The state of men's hearts also demands much in the way of uplift. Fortunately, the stated work of the pulpit affords opportunities for both teaching and inspiration. Ideally, the two qualities ought to blend in almost every sermon. At times, however, a man should aim deliberately to instruct. On other occasions he may think it best to inspire. If the weekly schedule allows two sermons on the Lord's Day, at least from September through May, he can do one kind of pulpit work in the morning and the other at night. In any case the plan for the year's preaching may well include a number of popular teaching sermons from one of the prophetic books. What a way to help prepare for the celebration of Christmas!

At present we are to think about such a popular teaching sermon. If the man in the pulpit knows his business there, he calls no attention to how he preaches. He can make a teaching sermon so clear and interesting, so helpful and uplifting, that the friend in the pew may scarcely

191

know that he has learned how to interpret and apply a portion from the book of Hosea or Micah. During the first few years as an interpreter the young minister should keep largely to the less difficult prophets, such as the first few in the preceding chapters. After he has learned how to work in a less difficult book he may attempt something harder, such as a course, or a series, from the first few chapters of Isaiah.

A course here means a number of sermons at the same service on consecutive Sundays, all on the same general subject, but not announced as a unified whole. A course may run longer than a series, which means a number of sermons as unified and progressive as the chapters in a book.[1] If a man has not the courage to attempt either a course or a series, he may prepare an occasional teaching sermon from one of these passages. In any case he ought to look on the prophetic writings as a prospector views a mountain range full of precious ore waiting for the man who knows how to dig.

The Choice of the Prophetic Field

At first a man may wander hither and thither, in quest of a nugget here and another there. Erelong he should determine to drive his stakes and start digging underground. Before he settles in any one spot, he may sink a number of

[1] For such matters see my *Planning a Year's Pulpit Work* (New York and Nashville: Abingdon-Cokesbury Press, 1942).

exploratory shafts. He can share with the people what he finds in these preliminary studies. Out on the West Coast an incoming pastor put his church on the map by a series of popular expository studies on Wednesday evenings. Recently he has led the people through the prophetic books, a new one each Wednesday. Now the people understand why he thinks of these books, with the Psalms, as the most important part of the Old Testament.

Years ago another young minister did much the same at the evening service, under the general title, "The Message of the Prophets for Men Today." Because of that series he has gone through life with a love for the prophetic writings. At various times he has devoted special study to one prophetic book or another, always to find that the inspiration came largely from that exploratory series. Out of it has come, indirectly, the present book. Here follow the ten subjects, a larger number than he would now recommend. Stop while the people feel eager for more of the same kind. Also consider the wisdom of omitting the prophets' names, so as to encourage finding the books.

The Prophets: Men Greater Than Kings
Elijah: The Prophet of Fire
Amos: The Herdsman from the Hills
Hosea: The Prophet of Forgiving Love
Isaiah: The Prophet to the Nation
Micah: The Prophet to the Common People
Jeremiah: The Patriot and Saint

The False Prophets: Hypocrites
Malachi: The Prophet of Revival
Christ: The Matchless Prophet

The present work stems from belief in the wisdom of digging down into one of these sources at a time. This Bible book method Alexander Maclaren followed during his later years, though not always with the prophets.[2] He had found difficulty in deciding about the text for each successive sermon, perhaps because he had many claimants for every such honor. At last, because of his wife's insistence, Maclaren began preaching his way through one Bible book at a time, always with liberty to omit passages here and there. In time he became known as "the prince of expositors." Maclaren began to preach this way after he had become a skillful interpreter. How should a novice commence?

Be careful about the choice of the first book. Select one that you can master without difficulty—also one that will interest and help the people in their present stage of biblical understanding. All through this book I have taken for granted what now I stress. In planning a year's pulpit work, and in deciding what to preach on any given Lord's Day, be sure to start with the needs of the men and women in the home community today.[3] Otherwise, as John A.

[2] See E. T. McLaren, *Dr. McLaren of Manchester* (London: Hodder and Stoughton, 1912), p. 224. His name is spelled two ways.
[3] See my *Preparation of Sermons,* chap. II.

Hutton used to declare, the man in the pulpit may keep answering questions that no one in the pew ever dreams of asking. That kind of sermonizing may seem scholarly, but why call it preaching? Preaching means the interpretation of the hearer's life today, in light that comes from God today, largely through the Scriptures, and also through the man in the pulpit.

If the interpreter knows the hearers and their needs, he can find among the prophetic books the very one that will enable him to use the truths of God in meeting the needs of his lay friends. Both in sizing up the situation locally and in selecting the part of Holy Scripture, a man ought to seek and follow the guidance of the Holy Spirit. Otherwise he may spend much of his time in the pulpit shooting arrows into the air. With this clear understanding—that the need of the hour in the community ought to determine the choice of the prophetic oracle—give the preference at first to one of the shorter, simpler prophetic books, such as Micah. Later in the season among the epistles of Paul, start with Philippians. At some other time, begin with the Epistle of James, I Peter, or I John. After a number of years you will dare to preach from one of the more difficult prophetic books, always with a view to the needs of the hearers today.

In such pulpit work a man ought to watch the course of the Christian Year. Then he will plan for only one course or series from the prophets every twelve months.

195

During the weeks before Christmas he may work from any of the prophetic books. How early in the autumn he should start must depend on how many sermons he wishes to preach before he turns from the Old Testament to the New. In dealing with Micah he will reserve before Christmas one or two Sundays for messages from the early chapters of Matthew or Luke. What a way to signalize the Christian meaning of the Advent season! The sermons will mean all the more if the minister asks the people to read in their homes the book of Micah and then the First Gospel, or else the Third.

THE WAY TO START DIGGING

With such a program in the distance a man should begin digging months in advance. For the study of this one book, Micah, the pastor may set apart an hour or two five mornings a week. First let him read the book through at a single sitting. If he does not see it as a whole, let him go through it again, without any stops. Then he can take it up part by part. In any recent translation he will find paragraph divisions. Better still, if he knows Hebrew, he can start there as a basis. In expository work, however, a man looks at a passage more broadly than when he exegetes a single text. That sort of pulpit work also has its place,[4] but not in the present discussion.

Theoretically, a minister ought to study his Bible daily

[4] See *Preparation of Sermons,* chaps. IV, V.

for its own sake. Practically, he will do so with more joy if he can use the results in the pulpit. He will accomplish more if he has in view a practical goal, but let him not think too much about all that for the present. Rather should he master the book of Micah as it stands. Near at hand he should have for reference a Bible dictionary, a historical atlas, and two or three first-class commentaries. Without such scholarly helps how could he make up his mind concerning questions of authorship and date? About all such matters an up-to-date minister ought to know what the scholars teach. He should also have opinions of his own.

These technical issues belong in the study, not in the pulpit. Partly for this reason, and to save time, they do not appear in the present volume. No book or chapter in the Bible was written to tell who wrote it, or who did not. Preaching from a passage in Micah, or anywhere else in the Book, consists in showing the hearer what the passage means in terms of today, and how he should live in its light. As an example of a minister who knows much about technical matters in the study, and does not mention them in the pulpit, take Dr. Raymond Calkins. For years he served as a pastor in Cambridge, Massachusetts, but he never became so busy as to neglect Bible study. Since retirement he has written a scholarly work, *The Modern Message of the Minor Prophets*.[5] Sometimes he takes what

[5] *Op cit.*, p. 126.

many of us regard as an advanced position critically, but in the pulpit he does not allude to matters of this kind. There he does nothing but preach, largely in terms of today.

Herein lies the path of wisdom. Once on a lonely road Philip the evangelist met a layman reading Isa. 53. The interpreter asked, "Understandest thou what thou readest?"

The man in the chariot replied, "How can I, except some one shall guide me?" Then the stranger turned to the passage and inquired, "Of whom speaketh the prophet this?"

Beginning right there Philip "preached unto him Jesus." Of course! The first thing first! What else did the layman ask? Probably that interpreter held definite opinions about the authorship of those words, and about the date of their composition. He might have spoken at length about theories concerning the Servant of the Lord. Instead of doing that Philip preached! Who follows in his train?

This man's way of speaking suggests another working rule. Whenever you can do so, throw the stress on one or two persons, not on abstract truth. If possible show each person in action, it may be in opposition to someone else. As soon as you can, translate action into terms of today. Get the hearer to think of himself in the place of that eunuch, and of the preacher as Philip. In short, appeal to imagination. Remember that an unimaginative discussion of such a dramatic scene would misrepresent the facts in the Bible.

A teacher of unimaginative young ministers often utters this prayer about a young man who needs to wake up: "Lord, open his eyes that he may see!" These words came from Elisha in the mountains at a time of peril (II Kings 6:14-17). Before this older man prayed, his young companion seemed almost beside himself with terror. Afterward he beheld the mountains full of horses and chariots of fire. All of which may spell the difference between the man who knows how to preach with prophetic fire and the one who contents himself with recounting facts as prosaic as cobblestones in a deserted street.

As a man with imagination George Adam Smith has become a favorite writer about the prophets. While still a young pastor he worked his way through Isaiah in a course of sermons that later found their way into "The Expositor's Bible." There and in the less striking commentary about *The Book of the Twelve* he concerned himself with the meaning of each passage in terms of the preacher's day, and with the difference the truth at hand ought to make in the life of the hearer. Whether or not all of his ideas win assent, they cause everyone to feel a desire to see and act, where many a dry-as-dust commentator would make one think of the pedant about whom Robert Browning wrote "A Grammarian's Funeral":

199

Before living he'd learn how to live—
No end to learning:

. . . .

This high man, with a great thing to pursue,
Dies ere he knows it.

. . . .

This man decided not to Live but Know.

Learn to see, to feel, to act! Herein lies the first truth many a would-be preacher from the prophets needs to learn. When he comes to the seminary, or turns to a book about preaching, he may demand: "Teach me a system that will enable me unerringly to unfold the meaning of any prophetic passage."

The teacher, or the author, can merely sigh as he says: "My dear young friend, only God can do that! He does it, as a rule, by opening your eyes to behold what you never have dreamed of seeing. As for the method, that depends on the beholder, and on the book. Only a dunce would deal with Micah as he does with Hosea." "Lord, open his eyes, that he may see!"

One other negative word! In working your way through a Bible book, if you come to a passage in which you can see no vision to share with lay friends, do not preach from that passage until you have seen your vision and felt your heart burn. Learn to select and to omit. If at present any group of sound words does not yield a message to uplift others, why attempt to pound out a sermon?

200

Even Robertson of Brighton or Maclaren of Manchester did not attempt to preach from every part of the Bible book in hand. On the contrary, whenever your heart burns with fire from God, you can set the hearer's soul aflame. Instead of becoming merely a "biblical grammarian," why not speak as one of the Lord's prophets today?

THE HELP FOR THE FRIEND IN THE PEW

Many of our hearers would profit immediately from such teaching messages. Other laymen might not at first seem responsive, but they would learn to enjoy the right sort of informative sermons. A few with "motion-picture minds" or a television tendency might not thank the minister for expecting them to think. If so, do not blame the laymen for such indifference. In some churches for two or three generations the people have been entertained with "inspirational talks," largely devoid of biblical substance or any intellectual content. In some other churches the hearers have enjoyed every Lord's Day a sort of Cook's Tour through the Holy Scriptures.

Some of our laymen may relish such pulpit fare, but others feel the need of a change. Take a federal judge who attended his home church every Lord's Day, and there did his part as one of the leading officers. After he had heard a teaching sermon far from home, he said with a sigh, "A man likes to bring his brains to church, and keep them busy there." He did not wish anything profound, but he longed for something to remember and live by all week. Similar testimony comes from former Dean Charles R. Brown of Yale:

It would be difficult to name any other serious work in all the world of serious activity that is done in such haphazard fashion as is the work of religious instruction from the pulpit. The moment a minister finishes his breakfast on Tuesday morning he realizes that next Sunday is coming. . . . "What shall I preach?" Ordinarily he is free to preach on anything in heaven above or in the earth beneath. . . .

I am a firm believer in well-constructed courses of sermons, which give the advantage of some useful system to pulpit instruction. . . . I have used, with growing satisfaction to myself, and with increased profit to my hearers, the method of expository preaching. . . . Personally I have found it best to announce no programme or schedule in advance. The Gospel train does not need to run with all the minute exactness of a Twentieth Century Limited.[6]

In the first venture of the sort a wise man does not start with one of the prophetic books. After the people have learned to enjoy teaching sermons from the narrative parts of the Old Testament, he may find them ready for the more difficult prophecies. If these messages come each year before Christmas, he can show that the Old Testament prepared for the New. In order to do constructive pulpit work a pastor needs more or less of a teaching

[6] See *The Social Message of the Modern Pulpit* (New York: Charles Scribner's Sons, 1912), pp. 34-41.

mind, with ability to plan for more than one week in advance. So he can impart to the work of the pulpit a spirit of discovery and adventure.

Preaching from the prophetic books should help to assure wholesome variety. Only a regular attendant at church can tell how often the work of the pulpit suffers from sameness. As Dean Brown says, the man who chooses sermon subjects according to his moods falls into the habit of playing all his gospel music with only one or two stops, whereas people have a right to hear the entire organ. In some cases, Dean Brown observes, they must listen to a jew's-harp. In order to secure variety a man needs only to live among the mountains with one of the seers and then come into the pulpit with a vision from God, in line with the needs of the hearer. If you appeal to his imagination, the message will never seem dull or lifeless.

Better still, this kind of pulpit work puts iron into the blood of the hearers. When they come face to face with God as they find Him in one of the prophetic books, they begin to search their own hearts. At home they start reading the Bible in the spirit of prayer. They also try to live according to the vision they have seen in God's house. If such a description seems farfetched, remember that it comes out of pastoral experience. Under the right sort of teaching ministry almost any congregation can enjoy a revival the year round.

Preaching from the prophets tends to promote everything for which the pastor longs: home reading of the Bible, habits of private prayer, regular attendance at church, readiness for soul winning, and support of world missions—not to speak of enlarged gifts for the work at home and abroad. If this sounds like a large order, look about you for a church that excels in these respects. At the heart of that congregation you will find a pastor who loves to meet the needs of his lay friends by preaching from the Bible. Such a teaching minister does not ignore the prophetic books, which constitute one fifth of all the Scriptures.

The Values for the Man in the Study

The values for the pastor also bulk large. He looks on the welfare of the lay hearer as of more concern than anything else relating to the minister. Still the leader of the flock must keep his own mind and heart in good trim. How can he do that more surely than by spending an hour each morning with one of the prophetic books, and by mastering it in the spirit of prayer? As a biographer Douglas Freeman grew strong through living with Robert E. Lee, and Carl Sandburg with Abraham Lincoln. So the Bible interpreter can gain strength and uplift by living with Hosea or Habakkuk.

A teaching ministry requires that a man have a study, rather than an office. In the study he ought to live, hour after hour, with one of God's noblemen. No one can dwell with Isaiah or Hosea day after day and not emerge at the end of the period with a more robust personality, and with more of prophetic fire. So former President Nicholas Murray Butler of Columbia University once wrote about knowing mighty men: "Their names, their personalities, and their achievements have been through life the base-line from which I have been in the habit of measuring the minds, the characters, and the achievements of other men." [7] This holds doubly true of the minister who knows and appreciates the prophets and their writings.

A pulpit interpreter must employ all his intellectual muscles. How else can he expect to comprehend the deep things of God and make them clear to the man who has never learned how to read the Bible for himself? Also this kind of pulpit work tends to win for the minister the respect of his people. As Charles E. Jefferson says, "A church likes to feel itself in the grip of a man who knows where he is going."

Such preaching goes far to keep a minister happy. The man who feeds his people out of the Book can keep growing year after year. He need never cross the deadline before he dies. If in later years he retires from the pastorate, he can enjoy the satisfaction of having done the Lord's

[7] See *Across the Busy Years, Recollections and Reflections* (New York: Charles Scribner's Sons, 1939), p. 4.

work in a way that assures His approval, both now and hereafter.

In short preach as you will wish to have done at the end of your years in the pulpit. Begin now to make ready. If you wish next fall to deliver a number of sermons from one of the simpler prophetic books, start now to prepare. In the course of years, by the grace of God, you may become a teaching minister such as Micah. Indeed, why not aspire to become like Habakkuk, or even like Hosea? As for the rewards, some of them appear in the words of a master teacher:

What has it all been for? For the knowledge that makes life richer, for the friendship that makes life sweeter, for the training that brings power to the task which is hard and high, for the vision that shall light your pathway like a pillar of fire, for the truth that shall make you free.[8]

[8] See L. B. R. Briggs, *Routine and Ideals* (Boston: Houghton, Mifflin and Co., 1905), p. 135.

RELATED READINGS*

THE PROPHETS AS GREAT PREACHERS

THE PROPHETS AS GREAT PREACHERS

THE PROPHETS AS GREAT PREACHERS

Bentzen, Aage, *Introduction to the Old Testament.* 2 vols. (trans.) London: Oxford University Press, 1949. A scholarly presentation, more conservative than Pfeiffer.

Davidson, Andrew B., *Old Testament Prophecy.* Edinburgh: Clark, 1903. One of the ablest older works in English.

Duhm, B., *Israels Propheten.* Tübingen, 1922. Many of the strongest books about the prophets appear only in German. Such works are not listed from now on.

Gordon, A. R., *The Prophets of the Old Testament.* New York: Doran, 1916. By a Canadian professor of yesterday. Popular in form.

Kirkpatrick, Alexander F., *The Doctrine of the Prophets.* London: Macmillan & Co., 1907. Scholarly, able, helpful.

Leslie, Elmer A., *The Prophets Tell Their Own Story.* New York and Nashville: Abingdon-Cokesbury Press, 1939. Popular work by a professor at Boston University.

Paterson, John, *The Goodly Fellowship of the Prophets.* New York: Charles Scribner's Sons, 1948. Popular work by a Scottish professor at Drew Seminary. Good working bibliography.

Pfeiffer, Robert H., *Introduction to the Old Testament.* New York: Harper & Bros., rev., 1948. The ablest work of its kind. Liberal, but seldom radical.

* These titles include only a few of many. The books with bibliographies point to other works of various kinds.

Rowley, H. H., ed., *Studies in Old Testament Prophecy.* New York: Charles Scribner's Sons, 1950. A symposium by scholars of ability.

Smith, George Adam, *The Book of the Twelve Prophets.* 2 vols. New York: Harper & Bros., 1929. Like his abler two volumes on Isaiah, the best-known work of the kind in English.

Welch, Adam C., *Prophet and Priest in Old Israel.* London: Student Christian Movement, 1936. Interesting treatment by an Edinburgh professor.

Young, Edward J., *An Introduction to the Old Testament.* Grand Rapids: Eerdmanns, 1949. Strongly conservative.

AMOS

Cripps, Richard S., *A Critical and Exegetical Commentary on the Book of Amos.* London: Society for the Promotion of Christian Knowledge, 1929.

Edghill, Ernest A., *The Book of Amos* in the series, "Westminster Commentaries." London: Methuen and Co., 1905. A useful series, based on the English Bible.

McFadyen, John E., *The Cry for Justice*, "Short Course Series." New York: Charles Scribner's Sons, 1912. Popular, by a scholar.

Sutcliffe, Thomas H., *The Book of Amos.* London: Society for the Promotion of Christian Knowledge, 1939.

Wolfe, Rolland E., *Meet Amos and Hosea.* New York: Harper & Bros., 1945. "A commentary in story form."

HOSEA

Brown, Sydney, *The Book of Hosea*, "Westminster Commentaries." London: Methuen and Co., 1932. On the whole a good set for a pastor.

RELATED READINGS

Cheyne, Thomas K., *Hosea*, "Cambridge Bible." Cambridge: University Press, 1884.

Morgan, G. Campbell, *Hosea, the Heart and Holiness of God*. London, 1934. Homiletical. One of the ablest books by this interpreter.

Robinson, H. Wheeler, *The Cross of Hosea*. Philadelphia: Westminster Press, 1949. A small book, scholarly, penetrating, suggestive.

MICAH

Copass, B. A., and Carlson, E. L., *Exposition of Micah*. Grand Rapids: Baker Book House, 1950. Conservative. Thorough. "A new commentary where commentaries are few."

Thurman, Howard, *Jesus and the Disinherited*. New York and Nashville: Abingdon-Cokesbury Press, 1949. Thought-provoking, provocative. An eloquent Negro pleads for a reinterpretation of our Lord and our religion.

Wade, George W., *The Books of the Prophets Micah, Obadiah, Joel and Jonah*, "Westminster Commentaries." London: Methuen and Co., 1925.

ISAIAH

Gray, George B., *A Critical and Exegetical Commentary on the Book of Isaiah* (Isa. 1–39). New York: Charles Scribner's Sons, 1912. Scholarly. Not popular.

Jefferson, Charles E., *Cardinal Ideas of Isaiah*. New York: The Macmillan Co., 1925. Sermonic. Popular. Topical, not expository.

Skinner, John, *The Book of the Prophet Isaiah*, "Cambridge Bible." Cambridge: University Press, 1910.

Smith, George Adam, *The Book of Isaiah*, vol. I., "Expositor's

Bible." London: Hodder and Stoughton, 1917. The best-known work of its kind.

Stalker, James, *The Preacher and His Models*. New York: A. and C. Armstrong, 1891. Homiletical counsels.

Wade, George W., *The Book of the Prophet Isaiah*, "Westminster Commentaries." New York: Gorham, 1929.

Whitehouse, Owen C., *Isaiah*, vol. I, "New Century Bible." New York: Frowde, 1911.

ISAIAH—CONTINUED

Delitzsch, Franz, *Biblical Commentary on the Prophecies of Isaiah*. Grand Rapids: Eerdmann's, 1949. A reprint of a famous work. Conservative. This translation not based on the latest German edition.

Jordan, W. G., *Songs of Service and Sacrifice*. London: Clark, 1924.

Oesterley, W. O. E., *Studies in Isaiah 40–66*. London: R. Scott, 1916.

Peake, Arthur S., *The Problem of Suffering in the Old Testament*. London: C. H. Kelly, 1904.

Robinson, H. Wheeler, *The Cross of the Servant*. London: Student Christian Movement, 1926.

Scherer, Paul E., *Event in Eternity*. New York: Harper & Bros., 1945. Inspirational. Topical, not expository. Most suggestive.

Smith, George Adam, *The Book of Isaiah*, vol. II, "Expositor's Bible." London: Hodder and Stoughton, 1927. The most popular of all his writings. Full of imagination.

JEREMIAH

Baughman, Harry F., *Jeremiah for Today*. Philadelphia: Muhlenberg Press, 1947. By a Lutheran professor of homiletics. Helpful and suggestive.

Binns, Leonard E., *The Book of Jeremiah*, "Westminster Commentaries." London: Methuen and Co., 1919.

Calkins, Raymond, *Jeremiah the Prophet; a Study in Personal Religion.* London: Macmillan and Co., 1930.

Gordon, T. Crouther, *The Rebel Prophet.* London: Harper & Bros., 1932. Stimulating. At times provocative.

Kuist, Howard T., *Interpretation.* Richmond, vol. IV, no. 2, "Jeremiah," pp. 322-41. Extensive bibliographies.

Meiklejohn, William, *The Prophet of Hope.* Edinburgh: Church of Scotland Publications Dept., 1949, 72 pp. For young people.

Morgan, G. Campbell, *Studies in the Prophecy of Jeremiah.* New York: Fleming H. Revell Co., 1931. One of his ablest works.

Skinner, John, *Prophecy and Religion: Studies in the Life of Jeremiah.* Cambridge: University Press, 1922. Often counted the best book about Jeremiah.

Stephen, Dorothea J., *Jeremiah, the Prophet of Hope.* Cambridge: University Press, 1923. Popular.

Stewart, Alexander, *Jeremiah, the Man and His Message.* Edinburgh: W. F. Henderson, 1936.

Welch, Adam C., *Jeremiah, His Time and His Work.* London: Oxford Press, 1928.

Habakkuk

Allport, Gordon W., *The Individual and His Religion.* New York: The Macmillan Co., 1950, pp. 99-121. An objective psychological study of doubt.

Browning, Robert, "Rabbi Ben Ezra." Many editions.

Buttrick, George A., *The Christian Fact and Modern Doubt.* New York: Charles Scribner's Sons, 1934.

Davidson, Andrew B., *Nahum, Habakkuk, and Zephaniah*, "Cambridge Bible." Cambridge: University Press, 1920.

Lewis, C. S., *The Problem of Pain*. New York: The Macmillan Co., 1944. One of the increasing number of books by the most popular defender of the faith.

Peake, Arthur S., *The Problem of Suffering in the Old Testament*. London: C. H. Kelly, 1904.

Stonehouse, G. G. V., *The Books of the Prophets Zephaniah and Nahum*, "Westminster Commentaries." London: Methuen and Co., 1929.

Tennyson, Alfred, "In Memoriam" and "The Two Voices." Many editions.

Van Dyke, Henry, *The Gospel for an Age of Doubt*. New York: The Macmillan Co., 1896. Well written. Still helpful.

Wade, G. W., *The Book of the Prophet Habakkuk*, "Westminster Commentaries." London: Methuen and Co., 1929.

EZEKIEL

Davidson, Andrew B., *The Book of the Prophet Ezekiel*, "The Cambridge Bible." Cambridge: University Press, 1892. Brief. Able.

Lofthouse, William F., *The Prophet of Reconstruction*. New York: Frowde, 1920.

Robinson, H. Wheeler, *Two Hebrew Prophets: Studies in Hosea and Ezekiel*. London: Lutterworth Press, 1948.

Skinner, John, *The Book of Ezekiel*, "The Expositor's Bible." London: Hodder and Stoughton, 1895.

Snaith, Norman H., "The Prophets of the Exile," in *Religion in Life*. New York: XIX, 1, pp. 83-91 (Winter 1949-50).

RELATED READINGS

The Mine for the Preacher Today

Calkins, Raymond, *The Modern Message of the Minor Prophets.* New York: Harper & Bros., 1947. Critical parts sometimes advanced. Homiletical suggestions sane and helpful.

Chappell, Clovis G., *And the Prophets.* New York and Nashville: Abingdon-Cokesbury Press, 1946. Popular sermons, not expository.

James, Fleming H., *The Personalities of the Old Testament.* New York: Charles Scribner's Sons, 1943. Biographical. Scholarly. Popular style.

Knudson, A. C., *Beacon Lights of Prophecy.* New York: Methodist Book Concern, 1914. Like the book by James.

Scott, R. B. Y., *The Relevance of the Prophets.* New York: The Macmillan Co., 1944. Interesting and timely, by a Canadian scholar.

Yates, Kyle M., *Preaching from the Prophets.* New York: Harper & Bros., 1942. Popular treatment by a beloved pastor, formerly a professor at Southern Baptist Seminary.

INDEX OF SCRIPTURE

INDEX OF PERSONS

(Roman numerals indicate chapters; Arabic numerals, pages.)

218

INDEX OF PERSONS

INDEX OF SUBJECTS

(Roman numerals refer to chapters; Arabic numerals, to pages.)

INDEX OF SUBJECTS

INDEX OF SUBJECTS